RYAN'S TRIALS

LINDA SHEPHERD

Run the race,
Linda Shepherd

OLIVER NELSON

THOMAS NELSON PUBLISHERS

Nashville

Published in Nashville, Tennessee, by Oliver-Nelson Books, a division of Thomas Nelson, Inc., Publishers, and distributed in Canada by Word Communications, Ltd., Richmond, British Columbia.

This is a work of fiction. The events, settings, and characters are not intended to represent specific events, places, or persons.

Library of Congress Cataloging-in-Publication Data

Shepherd, Linda E., 1957–
    Ryan's trials / Linda E. Shepherd.
      p.   cm.
    ISBN 0-8407-9681-1 (pbk.)
      1. Teenage boys—Prayer-books and devotions—English.
    2. Christian life—Juvenile literature.   I. Title
    BV4541.2.S44   1993
    242′.632—dc20   93-25995
                                                                          CIP

Printed in the United States of America
1 2 3 4 5 6 — 98 97 96 95 94 93

To Jason. Welcome home.

Special thanks to Mark, David, Jerry, and Debbie.

❖

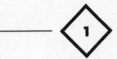

THE CLIFF

Let us fix our eyes on Jesus, the author and
perfecter of our faith.—Hebrews 12:2 (NIV)

*Ryan Stephens dug his fingers into a ripple of rock that creased
the glass-smooth cliff and inched his body higher. His free hand
groped above his head, searching for another fragment, a handhold,
anything to grasp. He felt a tiny crack.* Will it hold? *he wondered.*

*Ryan paused, his lungs aching in the high altitude. He clung to
the mountainside with only his feet and his fingers for support.*

*For a dizzying moment, he looked down, watching the earth spin
beneath him. Suddenly, the tiny rock crystal supporting his foot
broke loose, hurtling a thousand feet before smashing against a
boulder. Ryan's body plunged, then jerked to a halt.*

*Shivering, he hung from four bloody fingers. Slowly, carefully, he
pulled himself higher as his foot found a wrinkle to balance against.*

*Ryan hugged the cliff, his eyes squeezed tight against the rising
mist of evening. "I've got to keep moving," he whispered to himself,
"before my fingers freeze, before I fall to my death."*

*He looked up just in time to dodge a rock thundering past him.
Blinking, he stared into the orange glow of the sunset reflecting on
the mountain's face. He wasn't sure, but the mountain seemed to
be stretching higher. Ryan reached for another handhold.* It seems
impossible, *he decided,* but I've got to try.

A voice interrupted his concentration. "Time to get moving, Ryan," said his dad, already up and dressed.

Sixteen-year-old Ryan sighed as he rubbed the sleep from his eyes. *I hope that dream isn't a forecast of things to come.*

He poked his head out of the tent and watched his breath swirl into little ghosts.

Peering through the predawn darkness, he could see beams of flashlights bobbing up a narrow path. *It's only three A.M. and already others are on the trail ahead of us,* Ryan thought, shivering into his hiking clothes.

"Sky's clear," his father commented. "It's a good day for a climb."

Ryan studied the still twinkling stars and wondered. The Maroon Bells, fourteen-thousand-foot mountain peaks outside Aspen, Colorado, stretched above them like dark, forbidding giants. *Will we conquer them?* Ryan questioned. *Or will they conquer us?*

That dream and this hike have put me on edge. That and the fact that Kristi's along. Why didn't she stay home with Mom? He watched his fourteen-year-old sister sit up in her sleeping bag, tucked away in the warmth of their car.

It looks like she slept in her hiking clothes. That figures. She's too stubborn to miss anything.

Silently, the trio munched sandwiches, then Mr. Stephens helped Kristi fasten her pack.

"Ready?" he asked Ryan.

Ryan nodded, his eyes exploring the sleeping mountains. *It's now or never,* he thought as his heartbeat accelerated. *This hike will take everything we have and then some. Will we make it to the top of both peaks before the afternoon thunderstorms and back to the car before nightfall?* He fell into step behind Kristi and his father and determined, *We have to try.*

Lord, following You is often like climbing a mountain. It can be hard work, but the view from the top will make all my efforts worth any pain. Go before me and lead the way.

Additional Scripture reading: 1 Corinthians 9:24–27

❖

THE QUEST

Seek the LORD and His strength;
Seek His face evermore!
—Psalm 105:4

Rotten rock crunched under Ryan's boots as he stepped up the shadowy path. At first, he concentrated on the bouncing yellow beam of his flashlight, trying to stay on the ascending trail. Two hours later, his light faded in the glow of the coming dawn.

"Look at Pyramid," Ryan said.

The trio turned, gazing at the tremendous peak standing to the east. They watched its edges brighten with early sun gold.

Popping the top off his water bottle, Ryan offered Kristi a drink. "Not so fast," he laughed as she guzzled it. "We've got a long day ahead of us."

Mr. Stephens said, "It's five o'clock. At this rate, we'll make the top before noon."

"Maybe we'll get lucky and beat the afternoon thunderheads," Ryan said, reaching for his bottle.

He threw back his head to take a drink. All the while his blue eyes searched for the summit. *I can't see the top yet, but it's got to be there,* he decided. *I'll really believe it when I can plant my feet on it.*

Ryan topped his bottle and zipped it into his pack. *I guess discovering a hidden peak is like trying to know God. You can't see Him. You've just got to believe.* Ryan sighed. *God, if only I could touch You, maybe You would seem real, and maybe my faith would make a difference.* Psalm 105 came to his mind. *"Seek the LORD and His strength; seek His face evermore!" Yeah,* Ryan thought, *that verse describes my quest . . .*

His dad interrupted his meditation. "We've got to keep moving."

Ryan peered at his sister, noticing that her blue eyes were blank. *Maybe she's not awake.* He shuddered to think she might already be tired. *Well, she'd better hang tough!* he thought, silently mimicking the voice of his football coach, Bill Fite.

Ryan chuckled, *Coach would probably throw a fit if he knew I was taking my Labor Day holiday to conquer both peaks of the Maroon Bells.*

"Take the day off and rest!" Coach had said. "And above all, don't do anything stupid. Coach George and I want you back in one piece. We've got a big scrimmage coming up Friday against South Park. Rest up so we can win!"

Ryan studied the trail that meandered down the mountainside. It disappeared behind a large boulder. *What's on the other side? What adventures are lurking around the bend?*

Lord, sometimes You seem so far away I wonder if You're even there. Please prove Yourself to me, and teach me how to prove myself to You. Lead me in my quest to find Your truth.

Additional Scripture reading: Psalm 16:5–11

THE PEAK

For the LORD is the great God. . . .
In his hand are the depths of the earth,
and the mountain peaks belong to him.
—Psalm 95:3–4 (NIV)

It was really steep now, so steep Ryan could reach out and touch the spot that would become his next footprint.

I hate scrambling over rotten rock, he decided with a frown.

"Rock!" he yelled as his hand broke off a large chunk that bounced downward. He watched it topple out of view. Looking up, he dodged just as Kristi dislodged a fist-sized rock that whizzed past his ears.

"Watch it!"

"Sorry," Kristi muttered, speaking her first word in hours.

Ryan caught a glimpse of her face, trying to puzzle out her silence. He noted the determined frown that replaced her usually flapping jaw. *Kristi acts like she's trying to prove something.*

Maybe she is, he decided. *I was a little hard on her when she weaseled her way into this trip.*

"You'll just slow us down!" Ryan had complained. "We'll never make the summits and ridge. And if we do, you'll probably be so tired you'll walk off the side of the mountain!"

"At least I'll get to the bottom before you," she had quipped.

Ryan checked the position of the sun. It was almost nine-thirty. They'd been climbing for nearly seven hours. Again, he gauged his elevation by Pyramid. *We're almost to the top!*

Ryan's eyes traced the formation towering above them. "I still can't see the summit," he grumbled to himself. "The curve in the rock hides it from view."

Stopping his advance, Ryan said, "Hey, Dad, look! The trail's disappeared."

Mr. Stephens unlooped his rope from around his shoulders. "Looks like we'll have to use my rope, tie in, and belay the rest of the way. It's almost vertical."

"This way," one of the early flashlight people called. "There's a trail around this rock!"

Ryan scurried after them, stepping onto the wide summit. In the thin air, his heart pounded from the exertion of his wild ascent. *I made it!*

Before him, fourteen-thousand-foot peaks rippled across the horizon, looking like a storm-tossed sea of granite against a crisp blue sky.

Ryan sat on a nearby rock and thought, *So, there really is a summit to the North Maroon Peak. It's a good sign. If I can reach the summit of North Maroon, a summit I couldn't see from below, maybe I can learn how to reach God. There has to be a way to find the trail.*

Looking south, Ryan's gaze fell on North Maroon's sister, Maroon Peak. He studied the long ridge connecting the two. *No wonder so many people have died on that thing,* he thought. *It's a jagged trail of rotten rock and drop-offs. I wonder how Kristi will . . .*

Ryan turned to see Kristi scramble up the last section of rock, followed by their dad. She looked tired. A frown clouded Ryan's face. *Will Kristi be willing to try?*

He watched his dad pull off his Rockies baseball cap and ruffle his brown hair. Ryan wondered, *Will we attempt the crossover, or will we head down?*

Lord, thank You for being near, even when I'm not sure if You can even see me. Teach me Your ways, and show me the direction You have for my life. Help me to get to know You in a deeper way.

Additional Scripture reading: 1 Chronicles 16:8–12

THE GAP

I sought for a man among them who would
make a wall, and stand in the gap before Me
on behalf of the land.—Ezekiel 22:30

Mr. Stephens put his arm around Kristi. "Way to go!"

Kristi glared at Ryan. "Thanks, Dad. At least you believed in me."

"You did great, Kristi," Ryan said, standing and stretching his legs. "You're a lot stronger than I thought."

"You mean I've got my big brother's approval?"

"You're okay for a girl, I guess."

Laughing, Kristi said, "Thanks, I think."

"So," Mr. Stephens said, "are you ready to head back down?"

"Down?" Kristi asked. "I'd prefer to head south, to Maroon Peak."

"It's ten o'clock and the sky's clear," Ryan said, turning to his dad. "What do you think?"

Studying Kristi, Mr. Stephens said, "That half-mile ridge is treacherous. Are you sure you want to traverse it?"

"I'll be okay," she answered. "Let's go."

Ryan couldn't believe it. Kristi hadn't wimped out on him! *But,* he worried, *Broken Ridge is no place for a tired flatlander. Will Kristi really be okay?*

An hour later, the Stephenses were less than halfway across the narrow ridge, staring at a large crevasse. Ryan watched his dad stride across the gap with his long, lean legs. Kristi hung back, her eyes glistening. "Dad, I don't think I can make it."

Why do girls have to be so emotional? Ryan mused. *Although it is a shame,* he admitted, *Kristi's worked hard to get to this point. And there's no way her short legs can make the crossing unless . . .*

Ryan patted Kristi's back and said gruffly, "Kristi, watch this." Carefully, he kneeled at the edge of the crevasse and climbed inside. Straddling the space, his hands and feet pushed against the vertical walls.

"What are you doing?"

"What does it look like?" Ryan yelled. "I'm standing in the gap. Look straight ahead and cross over on my shoulders."

Ryan grimaced as Kristi's hiking boots dug into his flesh. Tentatively, she stepped over his head, carefully keeping her balance. A boot dug into his other shoulder as she pushed off, leaping toward Mr. Stephens's outstretched hand.

"Got her!" Mr. Stephens yelled.

Supporting himself with his feet, Ryan turned, grasping the edge of the far wall with his hands. As he pulled himself to the upper rim, a thought occurred to him: *Could it be Jesus had stood in the gap for him, the same way he had stood in the gap for Kristi?*

His dad caught his hand and helped pull him to the top. Mr. Stephens said, "Good job, Ryan."

Kristi gave him a hug. "Thanks."

Ryan smiled as he thought of his analogy. *It made sense. Until Jesus died on the cross for people's sins, people were separated from God, like the chasm separated Kristi from Dad. Just as I used my body to build a bridge, Jesus used His body on the cross to bridge the gap between God and humankind.*

Again, a smile darted to Ryan's lips. *There is a spiritual trail, a trail I can follow, the trail of the cross. And because I believe Jesus is God's Son and He died for my sins, I've already started the crossing.*

Ryan looked toward Maroon Peak. It loomed ahead of them. He wondered, *What obstacles will we have to overcome to reach the top?*

Jesus, thank You for standing in the gap for me. Thank You for being the way that leads to the Father. Show me how to make the crossing. Be my guiding light.

Additional Scripture reading: Romans 5:6–11

❖

THE BELAY

For you will be His witness to all men of what
you have seen and heard.—Acts 22:15

The next thirty minutes of the traverse were tough. *Broken Ridge's name is well deserved*, Ryan thought.

As they carefully picked their way across the fractured terrain, Ryan spotted what seemed to be an impassable roadblock. A twenty-five-foot cliff obstructed their path.

"Dad," Ryan said, "let me free climb this wall. I'll drop the rope down to you and Kristi and belay you as you climb."

His dad nodded in agreement as Ryan took chalk out of his backpack and rubbed it onto his hands. *I can't let my sweaty palms cause my grip to slip.*

Ryan stepped back and studied the face of the wall, mentally tracing out a trail of handholds and footholds. *Like my quest for God, this rock looks climbable*, he decided.

Swinging his body upward, he grasped a crack in the rock. He used a small stone outcropping for a toehold, pushing his body higher. As he climbed, time stood still. The ground, as well as Ryan's problems, fell away. He concentrated on his movements and the rock. *My problems back home seem ridiculous now*, he thought.

The silliness of his argument with his girlfriend, Brooke Kelly, and his competition with Jack Raymond for the starting quarterback position faded into handholds and footholds that pulled him toward the top.

Once there, he tied one end of the rope around his waist and dropped the other end to Kristi and Mr. Stephens.

Kristi tied the rope around her waist and shouted, "On belay!"

As she started up, Ryan thought, *Although I've helped Kristi once, it still feels weird to be responsible for her safety.* He frowned, watching her climb. *Kristi's slow, but at least she's making progress.*

"Oufff!" the air sucked out of Ryan's body as Kristi slipped. The full force of her weight cut into his midsection like a knife.

"I'm okay," Kristi yelled, trying to regain her footing as Ryan struggled to support her. When Kristi scrambled beside Ryan, he lowered the rope to his dad.

As Mr. Stephens climbed nimbly up the cliff's face, Ryan thought about his analogy of the gap again. *Am I responsible,* he wondered, *not only to make my spiritual crossing but to help others along the way, even when they fall?*

He looked at Kristi huddled on a rock. Both of her knees were skinned, but she didn't complain. She was too tired.

Ryan's stomach rumbled. *It's almost eleven-thirty. We'll eat when we make the summit.* He swiped his brown hair out of his eyes. *We've got a full day of climbing ahead of us. We can't go back now. We can only look up.*

As You lead me, Lord, help me to remember to include others. Show me ways to point them to You. Help me not to arrive at Your gates empty-handed, but help me to bring a friend.

Additional Scripture reading: Acts 26:14–18

MAROON PEAK

He has preserved our lives and kept our feet
from slipping.—Psalm 66:9 (NIV)

Ryan's heart pounded in his chest as he made the final ascent
to the summit of Maroon Peak. The view would have been spectacu-
lar if the clouds weren't already rolling around the distant peaks.
He looked at his dad and said, "It's only noon. The thunderheads
are early."

Mr. Stephens nodded. "We can stop here only long enough to
eat a sandwich and drink some water, then we've got to haul off
this thing," he said. "We don't want to be up here in a lightning
storm."

A few minutes later, the party started their descent. Although
the car was northeast of the Stephenses, the twist of the mountain
forced them to travel south, wandering through the clouds at thir-
teen thousand feet.

"It'll be a good two-hour walk before we can turn it around,"
Mr. Stephens said.

Ryan fell into step behind him, scrambling over broken rocks,
too tired to answer.

He frowned. Somehow, they had gotten on a lower trail, just
below some other hikers. *Won't these rocks stop falling?* he asked
himself, dodging yet another spray.

"Rock!" someone cried as a small boulder crashed down the
mountainside. Ryan ducked but not quickly enough. The rock
grazed his shoulder, causing his feet to slip beneath him.

"Ryan!" Kristi screamed, grabbing his arm to keep him from
toppling off the mountain.

Regaining his balance, Ryan tried to sound confident. "I'm okay."

He looked down the cliff he had almost tumbled from and felt sick. *I guess it was a good thing Kristi came along after all,* he decided. *Kristi and I helped each other.*

"Are you all right?" his dad asked.

Nodding his head, he rubbed the bruised shoulder of his passing arm. *It'll be okay in a few days,* he assured himself as the first boom of thunder rumbled around them.

The clouds were beginning to boil only a few feet above them, splashing rain against Ryan's cheek. "We've got to get off this mountain!" he shouted.

Life is full of dangerous obstacles. Put a hedge of protection around me and my family, and help me to stay on the trail. Please send Your angels to protect me, and give me strength not to falter.

Additional Scripture reading: Psalm 37:27–34

❖

THE DESCENT

—

When my spirit was overwhelmed within me,
Then You knew my path.—Psalm 142:3

As the rain beat steadily over the already soaked band of hikers, Ryan kept peering down the steep slopes. *If only we could get down and find a more direct route to the car. This backtracking's grueling,* he thought.

Again and again, he started down through a break in the rocks, only to be forced back when the lower trail evaporated.

He glanced at Kristi. *Her lips are blue, but she hasn't started to shiver. Keep walking,* he silently urged. *We can't afford a case of bone-chilling hypothermia.*

The sky was dimming. *We're still miles from the car. We've got to find a way back,* Ryan determined.

Repeatedly, Ryan and his dad and sister slipped on the slick grass and rock. *At this rate, we'll never make it.*

Finally, the trio stumbled upon the switchback they'd hoped for, a trail to the car. Ryan cheered, unable to make his voice heard above the rain and the wind slapping around him. *This would be a natural place to rest and eat, but we can't risk allowing our bodies to cool down.*

The slopes were steadily darkening as they half walked, half slid toward the northeast.

Ryan's shoulder throbbed. *Surely, it will be all right. It has to be. I can't let an injury force me to hand my quarterback position over to Jack. I've worked too hard.*

He smiled as his mind turned to Brooke, his girlfriend. She was a gorgeous cheerleader he'd dated since last spring. Their relationship seemed great, except for their recent fight concerning one of Todd James's parties. He sighed. *I'll try to make it up to her.*

Awakening from his thoughts, he noticed the rain had stopped, leaving a cool, soggy trail beneath them. In the twilight, he spotted something up ahead. *The parking lot!*

Ryan stared at Kristi. After fifteen hours of hiking, she walked like a shivering zombie. *This trail has ended none too soon for her,* he decided.

He rubbed his sore shoulder again. *I hope this trip hasn't been too costly. I guess I'll find out at tomorrow's practice if I can get out of bed.*

Lord, You'll always see me through to the very end. Even when the road gets rough and the journey is long, You are there with

me. Thank You that every trail and trial comes to an end.
Thank You for being there for me.

Additional Scripture reading: Isaiah 26:3–8

THE
COVER-UP

Blessed are those whose lawless deeds
    are forgiven,
And whose sins are covered.
    —Romans 4:7

Butterflies swarmed in Ryan's stomach as he tried to pop the kink out of his shoulder. An ugly purple bruise hid beneath his denim shirt. *What am I going to say to Coach Fite?* he wondered. *The truth? Sorry, Coach, against your orders, I went mountain climbing and hurt my passing shoulder.*

Ryan frowned. *No. Coach'll blast me with words that will make me wish I'd never even heard of football.*

Looking up, he couldn't help smiling as Brooke Kelly, dressed in her cheerleading sweater and skirt, breezed toward him. Her long dark curls flowed behind her like silk.

His pulse quickened. "How was your weekend?" she asked, her blue eyes searching his.

"The mountains were great," Ryan answered, putting his arm around her shoulder. "How was yours?"

"Boring," Brooke retorted. "Without you here to take me to Todd's party, I was miserable. I hear it was the party of the season. All the kids said they had a blast."

"Sorry to hear that," Ryan joked. "But I'm kind of glad I missed it."

"Why?" Brooke challenged, breaking free of his arm.

Ryan looked down, embarrassed. He knew he couldn't explain, but he groped for words anyway. "Well, I hear Todd's parties can get a little . . . wild."

A big hand clapped Ryan's sore shoulder as Jack Raymond intruded.

Jack winked at Brooke. "Ryan's an odd one, all right. He doesn't know how to loosen up and have a little fun."

To Ryan's dismay, Brooke giggled, "And I suppose you do?"

"Certainly," Jack answered. "I'd like to show you sometime."

"Jack, go home!" Ryan snapped.

"Touchy," Jack replied. "See? He's too serious. What you need is a real man, like me."

Ryan rolled his eyes and asked, "Isn't that your mother calling?"

"I was just leaving. But don't worry. I'll loosen you up on the field this afternoon," Jack said, smacking his fist into his open palm. "With a *splat!*"

As Jack retreated down the hall, a shadow loomed over Ryan and Brooke. Turning around, Ryan looked up to see Coach Fite.

Coach said, "I hope you're rested up for practice."

Ryan tried not to grimace as the coach patted his shoulder. "Yeah, I feel great," he lied.

Coach Fite disappeared into a classroom. *What do I do?* Ryan wondered. *Keep lying or confess to my bruise?*

Rubbing his shoulder again, Ryan decided, *I have the rest of the day to think it over . . . to decide whether I'll pretend to get hurt during practice or whether I'll come clean. But with Jack around, pretending to get hurt might not take much pretending.*

Teach me how to be honest, Lord. Guard my lips and help me to keep my tongue in check. I want to stay close to Your love, regard-

less of the cost. Cover my sins with Your blood, and expose the truth with Your light.

Additional Scripture reading: 1 Peter 2:11–17

❖

HIDDEN SIN

If we confess our sins, He is faithful and just to forgive us our sins and to cleanse us from all unrighteousness.—1 John 1:9

Ryan got to football practice early. He wanted to put on his uniform before the other players could see his purple bruise. Wincing, he gently fit his shoulder pads into place and reached for his jersey. The shirt felt stiff from last week's practice. *I'll have to wash it soon,* he decided, *before it takes on a life of its own.*

Is it my imagination, Ryan wondered, rubbing his shoulder, *or is my arm feeling a little better?*

He peeked under his shirt. His nasty bruise stared back at him. *Who am I trying to kid?*

Kicking at a candy wrapper, Ryan tried to decide what to do. *If I play poorly in practice, Coach Fite will replace me for Friday night's opener against South Park.* Ryan scowled. *If I confess my injury, I'll get blasted* and *have to sit on the sidelines . . . maybe for the rest of the season.*

Slumping onto the bench, Ryan stared at his feet. A third option was available. *I could try to play anyway.*

It would be risky, he realized, lacing his shoes. *I can't afford any more damage to my throwing arm.*

It isn't fair, he thought. *Here I'm trying to make God an important part of my life, and this happens. You'd think God would protect me.*

A thought crept into Ryan's mind: *Maybe not. After all, God knows everything about my life. He knows what's hiding under this football jersey. He knows all of my secrets.*

Could it be, Ryan wondered, *God's punishing me for . . .*

Ryan looked up as some of the guys jostled into the locker room.

"Hey, Ryan," Shawn Lively, one of Ryan's best buddies, called. "You're already dressed?"

"This guy loves pain," Jack interrupted. "He can't wait to see how I'm going to crunch him in front of his little girlfriend."

Ryan attempted to laugh. *Jack's words could be truer than anyone knows.*

Lord, my life is filled with so many choices that sometimes it's hard to know what to do. Teach me to hear and follow Your voice when I make decisions. Help me to know You are with me not to condemn me but to lead the way. Thanks.

Additional Scripture reading: 1 John 1:6–10

FAKING IT

Do not lie to one another, since you have put off the old man with his deeds, and have put on the new man who is renewed in knowledge according to the image of Him who created him.—Colossians 3:9–10

At the beginning of practice, Coach Fite studied his clipboard and announced, "In today's scrimmage, the second defense will play the first offense. Ryan will be the starting quarterback. Jack will play defensive linebacker. The rest of you, stick with your positions from last practice."

Ryan frowned. *This is the worst possible news. Jack will have a zillion opportunities to nail me. Can I endure his tackles?*

Pushing the question aside, Ryan joined the team for warm-ups. He was relieved when the coach went light on the calisthenics. It was hard to fake push-ups with his sore shoulder. The extra wind sprints actually helped him hide his problem. He sighed. *No one suspects a thing.*

As the team warmed up with a few laps, Jack was the only one able to match Ryan's pace.

He breathed down Ryan's neck. "Hey, Quarterbaby," he said, "you'd better save your breath. There's no way you can outrun me when the scrimmage starts."

A few minutes later, before starting his stretch-outs, Ryan took his right guard, Shawn, aside. "I got hit by a falling rock yesterday and hurt my shoulder," he whispered.

"What?" Shawn practically yelled. "Does Coach Fite know about this?"

"No, I'm okay," Ryan said. "I'll try to get by with less passing and a few more handoffs. You cover me, okay?"

"I'll try, but in this game, there are no guarantees. Especially when Jack's—"

"I know. Just do your best."

Ryan gave one last wave at Brooke before the opening kickoff. She and her cheerleading squad would be watching. He had to look good.

The aroma of the freshly cut grass filled Ryan's senses as he took his stance. A few yards ahead, Jack's glare burned into his helmet. Ryan called, "Red, two, three, hut, hut!"

The ball snapped for a blast. Larry Ware, the fullback, faked for a handoff, while Tom Timmons, the flanker, followed him, discreetly receiving the ball.

Jack Raymond pushed to the front line, but Shawn held him. As the action moved downfield, Jack broke free, slamming Ryan to the grass carpet.

The whistle signaled the end of the play. Tom gained five yards. Jack hopped up, wrenching Ryan up by his sore shoulder. Jack whispered, "Strike one!"

Ryan blinked hard and picked up the ball. *No matter what happens,* he decided, *I'll press on. Just like my walk with God, I've got to make it, regardless of the cost.*

Lord, I don't want to fake it with You. Help me to be honest with You about my problems. I'm not strong enough to fool You or the world. Coach my moves, and help me to press on in my walk with You.

Additional Scripture reading: 1 John 3:18–24

COMING CLEAN

Love does not delight in evil but rejoices with the truth.—1 Corinthians 13:6 (NIV)

Sweat trickled off Ryan's forehead as he leaned over the center, Ron Staley, for the snap. "Green, four, two, hut, hut!" he yelled after reading the coach's signals.

Grasping the ball, he ran backward for a sweep. He passed off to Larry while Tom ran interference. Larry made five yards before Kenny Salamon, a defensive tackle, creamed him.

At least, Ryan sighed with relief, *Shawn held Jack.*

Randy Morrell ran in to replace Larry and whispered to Ryan, "Coach says to give the ball some air."

Ryan swallowed hard and twitched his shoulder. He grimaced, pain shooting to his fingertips. *Concentrate,* he told himself. *You can do it.*

At the snap, he fell back, looking downfield for his tight end, Stan Fredrick. Ryan smiled, spotting his numbers. Then he noticed Jack. He had guessed the play and was racing to cover Stan.

As the defensive line rushed him, Ryan drew his arm back for the pass. The ball wobbled from his grip, zinging into Jack's numbers. Ryan's heart fell. *Way to go. It's an interception!*

Stan threw himself to the ground, his arms groping to tie Jack's feet, but it was too late. Jack bolted, charging toward his own goal line, free and clear. As he made the touchdown, Ryan could hear the cheerleaders scream in frenzy. "Jack, Jack, Jack's our man. If he can't do it, no one can."

The whistle blew, and Bill Brown ran toward Ryan from the sidelines. "Coach says to switch."

Ryan trotted back to the bench. *It's time to face Coach. There's no way out.*

"What were you doing out there?" Coach Fite asked as Ryan downed a cup of water.

Hesitating, Ryan said, "Sorry, Coach, I've got a sore arm."

"What!" The veins on Coach Fite's neck throbbed.

"A rock hit me on lower Maroon Peak."

The coach turned scarlet. "You went mountain climbing?" He turned his attention back to the scrimmage. "We'll deal with this later," he said.

Sometimes, Lord, it seems like everything I do is a fumble. Help me to gain some yardage and learn to follow Your voice. You alone know my heart; help me to keep it open to You.

Additional Scripture reading: Psalm 32:1–5

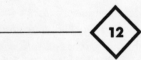

DISAPPOINTMENT

—

Why are you cast down, O my soul?
And why are you disquieted within me?
Hope in God, for I shall yet praise Him
For the help of His countenance.
    —Psalm 42:5

Ryan's ears still burned from the blasting he'd taken in Coach Fite's office.

"Stephens, what's the idea of playing hot dog up in the mountains?"

"I don't know."

The coach faced the wall. The veins in his neck pulsated. Abruptly, he turned. "I'll tell you what *you* are. You're arrogant! I *hate* arrogance! You're benched until Monday, the day I announce my final cuts. Because you have jeopardized this team, you may be off it!"

A few minutes later, Ryan squinted against the late afternoon sun. The field was deserted. Brooke was nowhere to be found. *Everyone is gone, except for . . . oh, no. Tagalong Kristi.*

"Hi, Bro. I saw what happened on the field today. Are you okay?"

"I don't want to talk about it," Ryan said, stuffing his hands into his pockets. He headed for the sidewalk.

"Is your shoulder still sore from that rock?" Kristi asked.

Ryan growled, "I said, I don't want to talk about it!"

"For what it's worth, I'm sorry."

Rolling his eyes, Ryan ignored her, although he felt sorry, too. *Only,* he decided, *the word sorry seemed like an understatement. Climbing the Maroon Bells had seemed like a good idea. Now it seemed foolish.*

What rotten luck, he thought to himself. *Jack's in. I'm out. As soon as I was benched, Jack passed for three touchdowns.*

Blast it, Dad! Ryan thought. *Ever since you split with Mom, four years ago, you promised me that climbing trip. And then, when we finally get a chance to take it, it ruins my life.*

Frowning again, Ryan asked himself, *Where's God in all this?*

Ryan thought of the summer camp, two years ago, up in Estes Park when he'd asked Jesus into his heart. *When will that decision make a difference in my life? When will I see some results?*

Lord, make a difference in my life. Help my life count for something. Show me how to know You better. Teach me how to hear Your voice.

Additional Scripture reading: 2 Corinthians 7:9–11

❖

HURTFUL
WORDS

In the multitude of words sin is not lacking,
But he who restrains his lips is wise.
—Proverbs 10:19

"It's probably for the best," Kristi said cheerfully.

The sound of her voice grated on Ryan's nerves. He was getting tired of her trailing behind him everywhere he went.

Kristi continued, "Things will be better tomorrow."

Without thinking, Ryan reeled to face her. He almost shouted, "No, Kristi, things won't be better tomorrow. I'm benched. I might be out for the season, and it's all your fault!"

Her mouth fell open. "My fault?"

"If you hadn't insisted on going on the trip with Dad, I wouldn't have had to knock myself out trying to make sure you were okay. I wouldn't have gotten hurt."

Ryan knew his words weren't true, but it felt good to say them. It felt good to vent his frustrations on his mosquito of a sister.

"I kept up!"

"In your dreams," Ryan retorted. "Those short, fat legs of yours slowed us down. You're a slug!"

She bit her lip, her eyes glistening.

They walked on in silence, a silence interrupted by soft sniffles.

When Ryan finally looked down at her, his conscience cracked. An apology began to form in his mind. Before he could say anything, a red pickup truck pulled up beside them. It was Jack.

"Hey, Ryan Quarterbaby! Or maybe I should call you Ex-Quarterbaby! Sorry about practice, but it was bound to happen."

"Get lost," Ryan seethed.

"What? And miss the chance of getting to know this cute babe?"

"Kristi's no babe!"

Winking at Kristi, Jack said, "Maybe you ought to get your eyes examined!"

Kristi half smiled, and Jack said, "You're not really with this clod, are you?"

"Are you kidding?" Kristi answered. "He forced me to walk with him."

"Then why walk with a clod when you can ride with me?" Jack asked.

"No!" Ryan shouted. "Kristi, don't get in that truck."

Kristi put her hand on the door handle and turned to face Ryan. "Try to stop me," she said.

Before Ryan could block her path, she climbed inside, slamming the door behind her. Jack's truck roared to life and lurched into traffic.

Ryan fumed as he watched the truck squeal around the corner and disappear. *How could I let this happen? Jack has the sleaziest reputation and the most disgusting brag lines of any guy on the team.* Kicking at a rock, Ryan sent it flying into the street. *Why did I have to say such mean things to Kristi? When will I learn to keep my big mouth shut?*

Lord, help me to realize the power my mouth has over my friends and family. Help me to say helpful things and skip the garbage. Teach me to encourage others.

Additional Scripture reading: Ephesians 4:29–32

WAITING

Flee also youthful lusts; but pursue
righteousness, faith, love, peace with those
who call on the Lord out of a pure heart.
—2 Timothy 2:22

Ryan checked his watch again and thought, *It's going on five-thirty and Kristi isn't home yet. If Jack so much as lays a finger on her, I'll . . .*

His mom called from below. "Ryan, did Kristi say when she'd be home? Supper's almost ready."

Tensing, Ryan called, "She didn't say, Mom."

Funny, I've never realized how important it is to treat a girl respectfully, Ryan decided as he paced his room. *But now that Kristi's out with Jack . . .*

Thinking of Brooke, Ryan sighed. *Things heated up between us the few times we were alone, but they never got out of control.*

His face burned as he imagined Jack touching Kristi the way he had always wanted to touch Brooke. *No wonder the youth director at church made such a big deal about premarital sex.*

"Look at it this way," Jeff Hoffman had said to the guys once. "Don't do anything to your date you wouldn't want someone to do to your sister or to your future daughter."

Ryan hadn't understood at the time, but now he was beginning to. He could see that pressuring a girl to get physically intimate was selfish and self-centered. *It makes a guy look like a big zero.*

His cheeks burned. *I'll be more of a gentleman with Brooke,* he decided. *I'll treat her the way I want Kristi's dates to treat her.*

Just then, Ryan heard Jack's brakes screech in front of his

house. He peeked out the window to see Kristi tumble from the truck. As Jack peeled away, Kristi ran into the house, bypassing their mom and heading up the stairs to her room.

Ryan intercepted her in the hallway and asked, "Are you okay?"

As Kristi looked up, he could see mascara streaking her face. She ducked her head and folded her arms, trying to hide the mismatched buttons on her blouse. "I'm fine," she choked, slamming her door behind her.

When it comes to girls, show me how You would have me treat them. Teach me how to treat them with respect and avoid situations too hot to handle. Teach me how to control my sexual urges.

Additional Scripture reading: Romans 12:1–2

❖

LOCKER ROOM MADNESS

Beloved, let us love one another, for love is of
God; and everyone who loves is born of God
and knows God.—1 John 4:7

The next day, Ryan was still fuming over Kristi and Jack when he got to the locker room to suit up for practice. Although he was benched, he still had to go through the warm-ups with the rest of the team.

As he yanked his shirt over his head, a jock strap zinged across the room and hit him in the chest.

Ryan peeked out from under his shirt before wadding it into a ball. Looking around, he spotted Shawn trying to hide a grin.

"Very funny, Shawn," Ryan said.

Touching Ryan's shoulder, Shawn said, "Ouch, ugly bruise there. Is that souvenir from the Maroon Bells?"

"Yeah," Ryan said, "it'll be better in a couple of days."

"In time for South Park?"

"Not unless Coach has a change of heart."

Before Shawn could respond, Todd bounded into the middle of the players. The overhead lighting made his blond hair glow. "Good news, guys! I'm having a kegger at my house after the game Friday night. Be there!"

"All right!" the guys whooped.

Jack, who had just entered the locker room, turned to Ryan and said, "Too bad you're such a stick in the mud, Stephens. You'll probably let this opportunity pass by, too."

"What's that supposed to mean?" Ryan snarled.

"It's like that little blonde babe. You had first crack at her, but she wanted a real man," Jack retorted, ripping off his T-shirt. "She turned out to be a lot of fun."

Hooting, Stan Fredrick yelled, "Is that who scratched your chest?"

"Yeah," Jack turned around, showing off his stripes. He grinned. "She played rough."

Before he could think, Ryan plowed his fist into Jack's gut, causing him to reel backward. Lowering his head, Ryan rammed Jack again, hurtling him into the lockers. "That was my little sister, you creep," Ryan shouted. "What did you do to her?"

A hush fell over the locker room as Coach Fite's angry face appeared around the corner. He barked, "You knotheads are *fighting?*"

Coach scanned the faces of his team. "I will *not* tolerate fighting on my team under any circumstances. The next players I catch fighting are out. Understand, Stephens?"

Avoiding Jack's eyes, Ryan nodded. *I'll have to wait to murder Jack until the season's over. I'll live for the day.*

Lord, some people really get to me. Help me understand what You mean when You say to love my enemies and to pray for those who hurt me. Love seems impossible to share with people who aren't likable. Show me how to follow You in this area.

Additional Scripture reading: Matthew 5:43–48

FABLES

For the time will come when they will not
endure sound doctrine, but according to their
own desires, because they have itching ears,
they will heap up for themselves teachers;
and they will turn their ears away from
the truth, and be turned aside to
fables.—2 Timothy 4:3–4

Ryan tried to shrink in his chair. *Sometimes,* he decided, *it's not easy having Fite as both my coach and my biology teacher. After yesterday's scene in the locker room, I'd better lie low for a while.*

At the start of class, Coach took a silent roll call. Ryan reddened as Coach's eyes penetrated him. Coach Fite snapped the attendance book shut and turned to write one word on the blackboard: E-V-O-L-U-T-I-O-N.

Out of the corner of his eye, Ryan saw Shawn raise his hand. Shawn asked, "Coach, shouldn't that be theory of evolution?"

Coach turned around and stated, "In my classroom, it's no theory. It's law."

Ryan noticed Shawn's grimace. *Don't blow it, Shawn,* he

pleaded in the quietness of his mind. *You're up for team captain.*

Even as the tension mounted, Ryan couldn't help casting an admiring glance at his red-haired friend. He was smart, maybe even brilliant. *And* he was a Christian.

Ryan knew Shawn loved talking about cosmology, the study of the universe. Shawn had told Ryan how he and his brother, a physicist graduate student at State, sometimes stayed up late discussing the latest developments in the field.

Ryan grimaced as Shawn ventured, "Even Charles Darwin, the father of the theory of evolution, said that if evolution were true, the fossil record would prove it."

"So, what's your point?" Coach asked.

"It's been well over a hundred years and the fossil record *still* hasn't proven evolution," Shawn answered. "As it is, only a few fossils are thought to be links between certain species. These claims are highly speculative, but nobody tells us teens that."

Shawn continued, "Science in the classroom is biased. Even our textbooks refuse to tell the truth. They leave out the relevant scientific data, some of which has been around for twenty years!"

Clearing his throat, Coach said, "Well, Shawn, if you're trying to give a plug to the myth of creation, you should know the law says I don't have to discuss it."

"Just because legislators have banned our ability to talk about God in the classroom doesn't mean God doesn't exist," Shawn countered. "Why don't our texts cover the Big Bang theory?"

Ryan laid his head on his desk and thought, *Shawn's getting in over his head with Coach. And when Shawn gets keyed up, there's no stopping him.*

Peeking out from under his arms, Ryan studied Coach's scowl. *How will Coach react to Shawn's challenge?*

Lord, my generation has been lied to more than any other. Our educators tell us there is no God, no Creator. They try to teach us fables that are said to be scientific but have little or no basis of truth. Lord, open our eyes. Let my generation find the truth!

Additional Scripture reading: Romans 1:20–32

THE
BIG BANG

—

> For since the creation of the world His
> invisible attributes are clearly seen, being
> understood by the things that are made, even
> His eternal power and Godhead, so that they
> are without excuse.—Romans 1:20

Ryan chewed his lip and stared at Shawn. *Will Shawn back down?*

"So, Shawn," Coach said, "since you seem to be an expert, what can you tell us about the Big Bang theory?"

"I just read about it in *Discover*," Shawn countered. "Scientists are gathering more evidence that the universe began with a giant explosion. They've discovered this explosion left behind a smooth, uniform layer of radiation throughout the universe. You can see this radiation in the fuzzy pattern your TV picks up when you lose your signal."

Shawn continued, "Not long ago, a group of scientists, who studied data gathered by a satellite nicknamed COBE, announced they had discovered tiny lumps in this otherwise smooth radiation flow. They believe these lumps are the very seeds of the stars and were generated by the Big Bang. One scientist said it was 'like looking at God.'"

The coach snorted. "It's not wise to mix science and religion."

"Maybe, but it makes you wonder," Shawn said thoughtfully. "The question real cosmologists are asking these days is not whether the Big Bang ever occurred but how. Maybe when our scientists finish scaling their mountain, they'll discover a theologian has been sitting on the top all along."

After class, Ryan congratulated Shawn. "Way to go. You really knocked Coach's socks off."

Shrugging, Shawn said, "I couldn't help it. Nobody tells us kids the truth anymore. I'm really fed up. I had to speak out."

"I guess I'm glad you did," Ryan agreed. "As long as it doesn't hurt your chances of making team captain."

"There's a chance I might not make it anyway."

"Do you know what's really exciting about all of this?" Ryan asked.

"What?"

"Even though science has tried to deny God's existence, the denial hasn't affected God. He's still where He's always been, sitting on His throne. Only the people who have their eyes open can see."

Shawn patted Ryan's back. "Too true," he said.

Lord, You are awesome. Thank You for creating the universe. Thank You for creating me. Help me to respect all of the other people You have also created.

Additional Scripture reading: Genesis 1:1–31

SOUTH PARK

You ask and do not receive, because you ask amiss, that you may spend it on your pleasures.—James 4:3

At Thursday afternoon's practice, while most of the team participated in a light scrimmage, Ryan threw a few passes to Eric Maxwell on the sidelines. Coach asked, "Do you think you might be up to playing tomorrow night?"

"You bet, Coach," Ryan said.

The next night, under the spotlights of the Summitview Field, Ryan sat on the bench. *It's funny. Now that I might go into the game, my stomach starts to churn. But yesterday, when I thought I was benched, I felt great.*

Ryan's palms sweated as he watched Shawn and Jack take their positions for the coin toss.

He closed his eyes, praying, *Lord, let it be okay. Help me look good. Help us win!*

Before Ryan knew it, it was fourth quarter and the score was tied, 14–14. Ryan frowned. He was one of the only players with a clean jersey.

Will the coach give me a chance to show what I can do? He touched his bruised shoulder. It was still a little sore. But it could throw a pass, that is, *if* he got to play. There didn't seem to be much hope of that now. The clock was running out, and South Park had the ball on the Summitview ten-yard line.

At the snap, the South Park kicker stepped back to try for a field goal. The kick was low. Kenny Salamon leaped to block. *Bam!* The ball smacked into his chest. He wrapped his arms around it and hit the ground. It was blocked!

The Eagle fans screamed wildly, and the coach tapped Ryan. "Here's your chance," he said. "Give it some air. We're counting on you."

On his way out of the huddle, Ryan waved at Brooke and prayed, *Help me, Lord. Let things go my way.*

Ryan wiped the sweat off his forehead, leaning over the center for the snap. He could hardly admit it, but he was afraid, afraid of messing up, afraid of getting hit.

He gulped before he called the play and wondered, *Will God help me pull out a touchdown? Will He help me make my team proud?*

Lord, You are the phenomenal God of the universe. Forgive me if I have expected You to jump to my bidding. Instead, may I wor-

*ship and praise You. But even though You are so great, You hear
my prayer. You comfort me and direct my path. Thank You.*

Additional Scripture reading: James 3:13–18

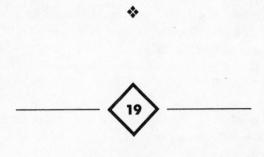

THE CHALLENGE

Let not your heart be troubled; you believe in
God, believe also in Me.—John 14:1

At the snap, Ryan rolled out to the right. Clutching the football,
he hunted downfield for a receiver and spotted number forty-eight,
Stan Fredrick, open to his left.

Ryan faked a look off, pointing his eyes to the right. As he did,
two snarling South Park linemen broke through the middle. Ryan
cocked his elbow, spiraling the football into the air.

Crunch! The linemen walloped into his body like a freight train.
Ryan's legs flew out from under him, and his head bounced as it
hit the field.

*When Ryan opened his eyes, he was staring into a blue sky. This
is cool! he thought as the noise of the football field faded, replaced
by a gentle gush of wind. He realized he was clinging to the side
of a monstrous cliff. He looked up. He saw nothing but a glass-
smooth wall of rock. He looked down. He could barely make out
the ant-sized trees at the cliff's base.*

"Help me, God," he prayed aloud. *"What do I do? Should I climb?"*

There was no answer except for the breeze that wrapped around his body.

Ryan decided to climb.

Tucking his football under one arm, he groped for a handhold. Suddenly, he heard his name.

"God, is that You?" he asked.

"Trust Me," a gentle voice answered in the breeze.

"How?"

"Let go."

Ryan looked down. The cliff fell for a thousand feet. He clutched the rock tighter. "I can't, Lord. I'll fall."

The gentle voice spoke, "I am with you."

The voice faded, and Ryan heard Coach Fite call his name.

"Ryan, Ryan, are you okay?"

Opening his eyes, Ryan found himself sprawled on the bench. Coach waved smelling salts under his nose. Ryan pushed it away and raised himself up on one elbow.

"What happened?" he asked.

"I'd say you got your bell rung," Coach answered.

Trying to sit up, Ryan asked, "The ball? Who caught the ball?"

"They did, chump," Jack said as he leaned over him. "You threw for an interception."

Ryan crumpled onto the bench. *I blew it.*

He rubbed his eyes, trying to shake away some of the cobwebs still clinging to his brain. As he did, his dream swirled to his memory.

Could God be trying to tell me something? he wondered. He shrugged. The dream didn't make sense. How could he let go when he needed to hang on, when his life was falling apart around him? He shook his head. He couldn't, he decided. He'd hang on for dear life.

Sometimes, Lord, I feel like I'm hanging on to my life so hard, I can't let go and give myself up to Your love. Teach me how to trust You. Teach me to invite You to go with me and to keep my feet from slipping.

Additional Scripture reading: Psalm 20:1–9

❖

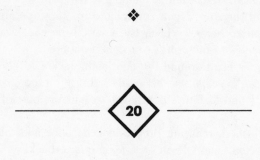

THE PARTY

But they also have erred through wine. . . .
They are swallowed up by wine. . . .
They err in vision, they stumble in
   judgment.—Isaiah 28:7

I can't believe I'm doing this, Ryan thought as Brooke and he walked into Todd's party, already in full swing. The music thundered around them, and Brooke waved at her friends, who were sipping their brews. Todd handed Ryan a whiskey mixed with ginger ale.

"Careful," Todd cautioned, "this might bite."

Taking a sip, Ryan wrinkled his nose. "I should probably pass," he said, deciding to take a stand for his faith.

From behind him, Jack laughed as he clamped a hand on Ryan's sore shoulder. Jack reached for the whiskey and said, "Let me show you how a real man drinks."

Jack popped his head back and polished off the booze in one gulp.

"Very impressive," Ryan said, faking a yawn.

Brooke turned to Jack and giggled. "You looked great on the field tonight," she said.

"So did you," Jack said with a wink.

Ryan pulled Brooke away. "The company's a little boring in here," he said. "Let's find something to eat."

Once in the den, Ryan rummaged up some peanuts while Brooke poured herself a beer. Ryan sat on the couch and stared at Brooke. *What's happening to us?* he wondered.

Poking his head around the doorjamb, Jack said, "There you are! You can't escape me that easily." He sat on the other side of Brooke. "I had to find out why you're hanging out with a loser like Ryan."

Ryan flushed, realizing Brooke looked concerned. She asked, "What do you mean? Ryan's the team quarterback."

"*Was,* you mean. Coach found out he couldn't take the pressure. At least, not like me."

"Ignore him, Brooke," Ryan said, trying to laugh. "Coach is just waiting for my shoulder to heal."

Waving good-bye, Jack blew Brooke a kiss as Todd appeared with another whiskey and ginger ale. Todd thrust it into Ryan's hand. "Drink up, Ryan, the night is young!"

Ryan washed down a fistful of salty nuts. *One drink won't really hurt anything,* he decided. *It may even help me relax so I can be a better witness.*

As he set his glass down, he fumbled to keep it from flying off the edge of the table. *See, I'm totally in control.*

Nancy Adams approached Brooke. "The bedroom is free now," she said.

"The bedroom?" Ryan asked in confusion. "You want to take a nap?"

Reaching for his hand, Brooke said, "I thought you'd never ask."

Unsteadily, Ryan allowed Brooke to pull him toward the bedroom door. "What are you doing?" he asked.

Brooke closed the door behind them and locked it. She wrapped her arms around him and steered him toward the bed. "Finally. I've got you all to myself."

Pushing her away, Ryan said, "No, Brooke. This isn't right."

Ryan staggered from the sting of Brooke's slap. Her blue eyes sparked fire. "Jack's right," she said. "You *are* a loser. You had a chance with me, and you blew it."

She stormed from the room and slammed the door behind her. Too stunned to move, Ryan sat on the edge of the bed and wondered, *What should I do now?*

Lord, thank You that temptation comes with a way of escape. Help me not to deceive myself into thinking I'm locked into situations that aren't from You. I renounce sin and evil in my life. Show me how to live for You.

Additional Scripture reading: 1 Corinthians 6:15–20

❖

SMASHED

—

Do not be drunk with wine . . . but be filled with the Spirit.—Ephesians 5:18

An hour later, Ryan sat slouched on Todd's couch, four beers under his belt. He didn't know where Brooke was, maybe off with Jack.

After all, he thought, staggering to the keg to fill his glass, *God let me down. I deserve a good buzz.* A familiar voice interrupted him, "Ryan! What are you doing?"

Turning to face Shawn, Ryan slurred, "I'm just havin' a little drink."

"How about going for a walk?" Shawn asked, guiding Ryan into the night air.

Ryan stumbled in the moonlight, then balanced against a tree. "Shawn, what are you doin' here?"

"I saw Brooke at McGuffy's with Jack. I had a feeling you might be in trouble."

"What about your big date with Jackie?"

"She wasn't feeling well, so I took her home."

"Oh."

Shawn pressed. "Did you and Brooke have a fight?"

"Yeah," Ryan answered, unwilling to reveal the details.

"So, is that why?"

"Why what?"

"Why you've been drinking?"

Ryan turned to walk down the sidewalk. "I don't know."

"I thought we had an agreement," Shawn said. "We'd skip the booze and concentrate on body and soul."

Ryan shrugged.

"Then why?"

Looking toward the stars, which were spinning overhead, Ryan said, "I was dumb."

"Do you realize you just filled your body with poison?" Shawn snorted. "I'm just glad you're not driving."

"I'll have to pass the driver's test first," Ryan joked.

Shawn studied Ryan's gait, shaking his head. "I'd hate to guess what your alcohol level might be."

"Alcohol level?"

"Yeah, they measure it by how much booze is in your bloodstream. You're impaired, at the very least. Maybe even drunk."

"Impaired? Is that bad?"

"If you were driving, you could lose your license or wrap your car around a tree."

"But I'm not drivin'," Ryan slurred.

"Yeah? Well, you broke the law anyway. You're under age!"

Ryan wasn't sure if what he felt was guilt or nausea.

He tried to gulp down the warm sensation rising in his throat. "Did you say alcohol is poison?"

"It goes straight into your bloodstream to depress your brain and weaken your spirit," Shawn answered.

Why did Shawn stop walking? Ryan wondered. Turning, he saw that they were standing in front of his house. His gut wrenched, splattering the driveway.

Doubled over, he decided, *Shawn's right. It was a terrible idea to drink.* He retched again. *Now, if only I can find a way to get into the house without Mom catching me.*

Lord, teach me how to get high on You and not on drugs and alcohol. They will only drag me down, but You will take me by my hand and lift me up. Teach me the joy of my salvation.

Additional Scripture reading: Romans 8:5–17

❖

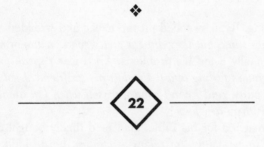

HOPELESS?

—

Now may the God of hope fill you with all
joy and peace in believing, that you may
abound in hope by the power of the Holy
Spirit.—Romans 15:13

Ryan's stomach rolled in waves of nausea. He tried to remember the night before. *Mom was hysterical,* he recalled. *Not so much because I barfed on her new rug but because I came home drunk.*

"We'll talk tomorrow!" she promised.

Tomorrow was now. Ryan refused to open his eyes. *Maybe today will go away,* he hoped. It didn't. He lifted a shaky hand to his throbbing temple. *What happened at Todd's party? Why can't I remember?*

Through the swirling fog, he pictured Jack laughing—the locked bedroom door—Brooke's slap. *Maybe I don't want to remember,* he thought. He turned over and flipped on his radio, listening to the announcer report another convenience store robbery.

That's the fifth Masked Bandit robbery this year, Ryan realized as his favorite song blared into the room. He listened to the words:

> *You're nothing but a zero!*
> *You ain't going nowhere.*
> *There's no place . . . left . . . to go.*
> *Give up, give in,*
> *You ain't gonna win.*
> *Cause hopeless . . . is all you know.*

Frowning, Ryan switched off the music and wrinkled his nose. *Those lyrics stink, but they draw a pretty good picture of me.*

He mentally listed his problems: *Kristi won't speak to me. My football game's falling apart. I've lost my girlfriend. I got smashed at Todd's party. And I can't control myself when I'm alone.*

Lord, is there any hope?

Ryan reached for his Bible, glad he'd finally bought a version he could understand. *I'm taking a chance,* he decided, *but I'm desperate. And who knows? Maybe I'll find something that will help me understand what's going on.* Closing his eyes, he flipped his Bible open to Jeremiah.

He peeked at a crisp page. Slowly, the text came into focus. *What's this?* he wondered. He silently read, *For I know the thoughts that I think toward you, says the LORD, thoughts of peace and not of evil, to give you a future and a hope. Then you will call upon Me and go and pray to Me, and I will listen to you. And you will seek Me and find Me, when you search for Me with all your heart. Jeremiah 29:11–13.*

His eyes widened. *Is the Lord trying to tell me that despite my failures, I'm loved and have a hope and a future?*

Maybe, he decided, *but I'll have to straighten up my life before I seek the Lord too much. The Lord might change His mind if He sees me up close.* Ryan determined, *I'll try to be perfect.*

Snapping his Bible shut, Ryan checked the clock. It was almost noon. He could hear his mother in the kitchen. *I can't hide up here any longer. I've got to face her.*

Lord, help me realize my life is not hopeless. Even though I'm far from perfect, You offer me forgiveness. Help me resist the temptation to strive for perfection apart from Your love and care.

Additional Scripture reading: Romans 5:1–5

❖

THE WRATH OF MOM?

—

Wine is a mocker,
Strong drink is a brawler,
And whoever is led astray by it
is not wise.—Proverbs 20:1

Ryan shuffled into the kitchen.

Mrs. Stephens wiped her hands on a dishtowel and studied him. "You look terrible!"

"That's how I feel," he admitted, gently rubbing his churning stomach.

He pulled up a chair and flopped down at the kitchen table with his head between his hands. "Mom, for what it's worth, I'm really sorry."

"I still want to know why," his mom said, sitting across from him.

Shrugging, Ryan tried to change the subject. "Did you know I might have lost my position on the squad?"

Mrs. Stephens refocused. "So, is that it?" she asked. "You were trying to drown your sorrows?"

Ryan shrugged again. "Maybe," he said.

"Did it help?"

"Not really. It just gave me a new set of problems . . . like . . . how to get home, how to handle my hangover, and," he smiled, "how to remove carpet stains."

He relaxed when his mom smiled back. But her smile quickly faded. "Are you planning to drink again?" she asked.

Shaking his head, he answered, "It isn't worth it."

Ryan fumbled with the salt shaker. "So, what are you going to do? Am I grounded?"

His mom drummed her fingers on the table and answered, "You're on probation. Next time I'll ground you for a month."

Ryan sighed with relief. "Don't worry, Mom. There won't *be* a next time."

Ducking his head, Ryan avoided her eyes. He cleared his throat. "Mom, can I ask you a question?"

"Sure."

"What does it mean when God doesn't answer our prayers?"

His mom's blonde eyebrows shot up. "Now, *that's* a hard one," she answered. "It's a question that I've struggled with for years, but I think I'm finally beginning to understand. There are reasons why some of our prayers seem to go unanswered."

"Like what?"

"Well, for example," she said, her blue eyes softening, "take your dad and me. When he left, I prayed he'd come home. He didn't. But I've come to realize that was his choice. God wasn't going to force him to change his heart."

"So, God's not responsible for choices made by others?"

"No. He gives us free will."

"Well, what about other kinds of unanswered prayer?"

"Like what?"

Ryan's lips hinted at a smile. "Well, like, let's say a football player prays for a touchdown pass but throws for an interception."

Mrs. Stephens's eyes twinkled. "That's a compounded problem."

"What do you mean?"

"Well, suppose someone on the other team is asking God for an interception?"

Laughing, Ryan rubbed his aching head. "I hadn't thought of that."

His mother continued, "There are times when God says wait or no. Although the reason may be hard to understand, God, in His farseeing wisdom, may know of hidden danger. Or maybe God knows your timing is off or your prayer is something that will eventually harm or hurt you."

Ryan nodded. "That makes sense," he said.

Teach me how to pray in Your will. Help my prayers not to be selfish or self-centered. Give me the ability to accept a no when it comes my way. Thank You for caring enough to listen to me.

Additional Scripture reading: Romans 14:13–21

❖

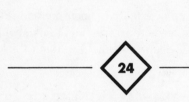

A NEW SONG

Sing to Him a new song;
Play skillfully with a shout
of joy.—Psalm 33:3

That night, Ryan watched as Shawn rumbled his decade-old car to a stop in front of the house.

"Bye, Mom," Ryan called, grabbing his denim jacket. "I'll see you after youth group."

He slid into the seat as Shawn slipped a Christian rock tape into his cassette deck. "Feeling better?" Shawn asked.

Ryan shrugged, listening to the music. The air pulsated as the singer sang,

> *Jesus gives you hope!*
> *Jesus gives you life!*
> *Jesus holds your future.*
> *He will get you through!*

The words are different from those I heard on the radio this morning, Ryan realized with a smile.

Turning to Shawn, he said, "I'm still feeling a little shaky." He looked around. "So, where's Jackie?"

"She's still not feeling well," Shawn explained. "She thinks she may have a touch of the stomach flu."

"That's too bad," Ryan sympathized.

"How's Kristi doing?" Shawn asked. "I didn't see her in the stands yesterday."

"She's still shook up over that argument we had. Plus, I think Jack upset her," Ryan answered. "She won't talk about it."

Staring at the road, Shawn asked, "You don't think Jack hurt her, do you?"

"If he did, I'll kill him."

Shawn was silent. "That dude needs the Lord."

"Yeah . . . or a prison cell."

"I couldn't believe it when I saw him with Brooke last night. She was your date. What happened?"

Ryan shook his head. "Don't ask."

A few minutes later, Ryan found himself tapping his toes. He thought, *This is amazing. When I got into the car, I felt down, but Shawn's music is pulling me up.*

"Great tape!" Ryan exclaimed.

"Yeah. I'm reprogramming my music diet," Shawn said. "Listening to this music is better than getting a buzz. Plus, there's no morning-after hangover!"

Groaning, Ryan held his head. "That sounds great. Maybe I'll reprogram my music, too," he said.

Shawn laughed. "Do what I do—a Christian tape and a Scripture first thing in the morning make my day go a lot better."

Ryan's mouth fell open. "You read your Bible?"

"I just finished Proverbs and now I'm reading James. I only read a verse or two. But it gives me something to chew on."

"Cool," Ryan said as they pulled into the church parking lot. "I'll have to try it."

Shawn turned off the ignition and put his hand on Ryan's shoulder. "Listen, I'm sorry about you and Brooke. But you know, maybe it's for the best. Maybe you'll see a girl tonight you'll want to meet."

"Don't worry," Ryan laughed, watching a girl enter the building. "I'm already scouting out the situation."

Lord, I give my music to You. Guide me to the Rock who gives me hope. Lead me to friends who will encourage me in my walk, and help me to get Your Word into my brain. Thanks.

Additional Scripture reading: Psalm 40:1–5

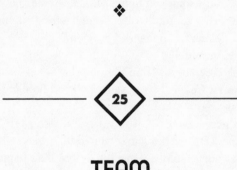

25

TEAM CUTS

**But for him who is joined to all the living
there is hope, for a living dog is better than
a dead lion.—Ecclesiastes 9:4**

Monday afternoon, the guys crowded around the roster, looking to see who'd gotten the ax. Ryan's heart fluttered as the guys screamed in agony or yelled in relief. Pushing a little closer, Ryan thought, *No one's offered me condolences yet. That's a good sign.*

Slowly, he wormed his way to the front. When he saw his name, he crowed.

Sneering, Jack turned and said, "I wouldn't celebrate just yet. You may be on the team, but I'm the new quarterback."

Ryan ignored him. *What Jack says might be true, but as long as my name's on the roster, I still have a chance to play.*

"Way to go!" Shawn yelled from across the room. Ryan wriggled out of the crowd to share a high-five. Before their palms slapped, Coach stepped out of his office.

He said, "Stephens, come in here."

Tentatively, Ryan stepped inside. *Am I benched?* he wondered. His heart pounded in his chest.

Feeling apprehensive, he sat down in a hard wooden chair across from Coach's desk.

Coach Fite stared at Ryan with a cold glare. "I'm giving you another chance, Stephens," he finally confided. "I know you're a good athlete. But I want you to hear this from me. Jack will be my starting quarterback. You'll play second string to him but first string in the defensive linebacker position."

Ryan nodded mutely.

The coach continued, "Don't let me down."

"Don't worry, Coach," Ryan said, his head bobbing like a buoy in rough seas.

"You're the one who needs to worry," Coach said. "I invited a couple of the scrubs, the guys who didn't make the team, to breathe over your shoulder. They'll be more than happy to step in if I need to pull you out."

Dazed, Ryan left the office and sat down on the bench. *So, Jack and I are trading places.* He frowned. *I was set on playing quarterback. Can I hack being a linebacker?* A mischievous smile played across his lips. *Then again,* he decided, *playing linebacker might not be so bad. I'll get to cream Jack at practice.*

He rubbed his shoulder. It was still a little sore. *I'll have to hold back a little until I finish healing up.* His frown deepened. *I can't hold back too much, though. Coach'll cut me.*

Ryan sighed in relief. *Even so, things may be getting better,* he decided. *Soon, I'll be able to drive, and maybe I'll even win back my quarterback position. There's always a chance.*

Lord, thank You for all the opportunities You give me. Help me not to blow it. Help me do my best not only for myself but also for You.

Additional Scripture reading: Philippians 4:11–13

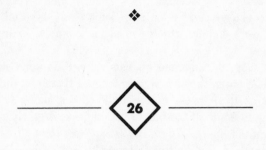

NERVES!

Come to Me, all you who labor and are heavy
laden, and I will give you rest.—Matthew 11:28

It had been a tough week. In practice, Ryan had nailed Jack whenever possible but never as hard as he should have. His game seemed slack, probably because of his fear of reinjuring his stiff shoulder.

I've got to buck up, Ryan decided as he suited up for Friday's game. *I've got to push through the line.*

Ryan's stomach did flip-flops as he rolled his shoulder. *It still hurts. How much more damage will it take before I'm benched for life?*

Stretching on the sidelines, Ryan tried to remember all the things Coach had said about Lamar High's team. *They're rated number two in their conference. Their game films showed their last opponents looking like road kill.*

Ryan thought of Lamar's quarterback, known by the press as the Bulldog. *I'll have to watch out for him. He's got a knack for getting the ball downfield, by air or by ground. He's tough.*

He took his position on the field and growled softly, trying to summon his courage. *When the ball snaps,* he thought nervously, *I'll look for an opening and cream the Bulldog. My career depends on it.*

He watched Lamar's center, a pimple-faced guy named Weaver. As the Bulldog barked commands, Ryan concentrated. *I'll do whatever it takes,* he decided.

His first chance came a few plays later. Ryan keyed off from the tilt of Weaver's helmet. *It'll be to the left, maybe for a fake,* he guessed.

At the snap, he slammed his fists against Weaver's shoulders, pushing him out of the way. Weaver fell and Ryan tore through the line. Just as Ryan guessed, the Bulldog was faking to the left, pretending to hand off the ball to his fullback. *Aha!* Ryan thought with a sprint of energy. *The Bulldog's still got the ball!*

Ryan charged, but the Bulldog straight-armed him in the shoulder. *Thud!* Wincing in pain, Ryan twisted his body away from the Bulldog's open palm, throwing himself for a cross tackle. As he dove into the Bulldog's thighs, his arms locked around the Bulldog's waist, dragging him to the ground. *Bam!*

The crowd went wild. But amidst the cheering, Ryan knew he'd been lucky. He trotted to the sidelines for a quick drink of water.

I have to relax and get into the game, he lectured himself as his trembling hand sloshed water from a paper cup. *I've got to quit worrying about my shoulder.*

Lord, even when I try to act tough, sometimes I'm afraid—afraid of failing, afraid of losing my way. Lord, help me to give my goals and dreams to You. Take charge of my life, so I can trust my steps to You.

Additional Scripture reading: John 14:25–28

BREAKTHROUGH!

The fear of man brings a snare,
But whoever trusts in the LORD shall be
safe.—Proverbs 29:25

Ryan checked the scoreboard. It was 7–3, Summitview's favor. The final two minutes were ticking down with Lamar possessing the ball at the Summitview twenty-five-yard line.

So far, I've played well, Ryan thought to himself. *I've helped hold the Bulldog at bay.* He frowned. *Can I do it for two more minutes?*

At the snap, the Bulldog passed to his flanker, Carl Redding, who broke through Summitview's defensive line. Ryan was hot on his trail. *I've got to stop him!* With a burst of desperation, he leaped into the air, zapping Redding for a tackle. *Whop!*

Ryan lay in the grass, his arms twisted around Redding's legs. At the whistle, Ryan struggled to stand. He tried not to stagger as he walked away. He felt beat, wasted. His shoulder throbbed. His lip was busted, and he was working on a king-sized headache.

He watched the referees measure the yardage. *Rats, Lamar's made another first down. Will they go for a goal?* The gleam in the Bulldog's eyes told Ryan the answer. *The Bulldog's going for 6 . . . 6 points that could upset our lead!*

Ryan got into position for the snap on the fifteen-yard line. *Which way will they go? Up the middle? To the left?*

Weaver's helmet bore straight ahead. *The football will fly,* Ryan guessed. *And when it does, I'll be ready. I'll crash through the front line and beeline for the Bulldog!*

When the ball snapped, Ryan danced in a bullfight against Weaver before breaking through. *I'm right!* Ryan cheered himself. As the Bulldog cocked his elbow, Ryan rushed him from the middle. Ryan lunged, bracing for the impact, yet at the same time, holding back. He watched as the Bulldog twisted away, completing his pass to Redding. Redding ran for ten before he was nailed by the Eagles' own Kenny Salamon.

Panting, Ryan lay in the grass. *I fell short! Does the coach suspect why?*

Again, Ryan prepared for the snap, this time on the five. *With thirty seconds left to go, anything could happen.*

While the Bulldog called the signals, Ryan's eyes fastened on Weaver. Weaver's face told the secret. *The Bulldog's planning to run the ball in himself!*

When play resumed, Ryan lowered his head, bracing for the impact. He rammed the Bulldog's chest. *Whack!* The Bulldog crunched Ryan's shoulder with his own. Ryan buckled, and the Bulldog slipped by for a touchdown!

The people in the stands screamed in frenzy, and Ryan melted to the turf. *That's my worst foul-up of the night,* Ryan chided himself.

Standing up, Ryan pulled off his helmet, pushing through the celebrating Lamar Hawks as the clock ran out.

He caught Coach Fite's eyes. *Does Coach know I chickened?*

Lord, sometimes I can't make it in my own strength. I get too beat up. I get too afraid. I give my life to You. Please walk with me, and help me to hold up under what the world throws my way. Thanks.

Additional Scripture reading: 1 John 4:15–21

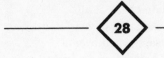

FORGOTTEN PRAYER

The prayer of the upright is His delight.—Proverbs 15:8

The locker room had been quiet, too quiet. The silence packed more guilt on Ryan's already sore shoulder.

Shawn slapped his back. "Don't worry about it. You did your best."

Did I really? Ryan wondered. *It wasn't just the pain in my shoulder that caused me to hold back. It was the pain in my heart. Does it show?*

Heading for the door, Ryan started his walk home. Todd stopped him. He said, "You're coming to my party, aren't you?"

"Your last party almost got me grounded. I'm still trying to get the stains out of my mom's new carpet," Ryan said with a grin.

"You're always joking, Stephens. So, are you coming?"

Ryan shook his head. "I've got my driver's test in the morning." He was glad he had an excuse Todd could understand.

Punching Ryan's arm, Todd said, "Don't lose any sleep over it. You'll do great if you don't chicken!"

What's that supposed to mean? Ryan wondered with a frown.

Ryan headed out the door, just in time to see Jack peel out of the parking lot with Brooke by his side. He stepped back into the shadows, sighing. *Maybe losing Brooke was for the best, but it still hurts.*

When Ryan arrived home, he found his mom and Kristi watching a classic movie on video.

"How did it go?" Mrs. Stephens asked as Kristi quietly slipped from the room.

"We lost, 9–7," Ryan said.

"So your prayers went unanswered?"

"No," Ryan said. "I didn't pray at all."

"What?" his mother asked. "Why not?"

"I didn't want to be disappointed again."

"Well, just because God might say no doesn't mean you should stop praying," Mrs. Stephens said.

"Besides," she continued, "you could have given the game to God, played your best for Him, and asked Him for special protection."

"I could do that?"

"Sure," Mrs. Stephens said. "Try it next time. You don't have to win every game to enjoy knowing God is with you."

"That's an interesting idea," Ryan admitted. "I wish I'd prayed that before kickoff."

"There's always next time."

Lord, thank You that You know my every thought and listen to my prayers. Thank You that I can come to You. Teach me how to pray and help our relationship grow closer. Teach me to recognize Your voice.

Additional Scripture reading: James 1:2–8

❖

ACCIDENTAL PARKING

For whatever is born of God overcomes the
world.—1 John 5:4

The clock radio burst to life, blasting Christian rock into the room. Ryan lay in bed listening.

> *Get an attitude check!*
> *And check into Jesus!*
> *He'll change your mind*
> *As He changes your heart!*

His eyes flitted to the window, analyzing the light peeking through the cracks of his blinds. *It's bright,* he decided. *It's going to be a nice day.*

An hour later, armed with his beginner's permit, he climbed behind the wheel of the car beside his mom.

She tightened her seat belt.

"Don't worry," Ryan said. "You've ridden with me enough by now to know that I'm a good driver."

Mrs. Stephens laughed nervously. "I hope so. I can't afford a new car right now," she said.

"I'll be careful," Ryan pledged.

"If you can establish a good driving record, I'll be more apt to lend you the car keys. If not, you'll have to walk."

"How am I going to get a good record unless I get to drive?" Ryan teased.

"That's a problem all right," his mom admitted with a grin. "Driving *is* serious. A car is basic transportation or a deadly weapon. You'll have to watch out for the other guy and never drive under the influence . . ."

Ryan groaned, "Aw, Mom, I got that lecture in my driver's ed class last spring."

A few minutes later, Ryan dropped his mother off at the Department of Public Safety's waiting room. He pulled his car into a line of mostly teens, all waiting to be tested.

Rolling down his window, Ryan enjoyed the morning breeze. He tried to focus on his upcoming maneuvers. *I can't go around those corners too fast, and I've got to concentrate when I parallel park.*

His stomach rolled with nervousness, and he tried to pop the kink out of his shoulder. *I've got to relax!*

Suddenly, his attention riveted to the car in front of him as an officer approached the woman sitting behind the wheel. She opened her door.

"Ma'am," the officer said, "you'll need to move to the parking lot. This line is reserved for people taking the driver's test."

Ryan's heart skipped a beat. *That means I'm next.*

As the woman revved her car engine, she reached across with her right hand to shut her door, accidentally knocking her car into reverse.

The officer leaped for safety as she shot backward. Ryan slammed the brakes of his parked car. *Crunch!*

That woman hit me! Ryan continued to jam the brakes. *I'm not even out of the driveway, and I've already had an accident!*

Too shocked to move, Ryan wondered, *What am I going to tell Mom?*

As he stared, the woman's little girl asked, "Mom, does our car look as bad as that boy's car?"

Ryan felt sick. He pushed open the door and stumbled out. His mom's headlight lay shattered on the ground. He walked back to the building. *How will Mom react? This just isn't fair!*

Lord, sometimes life is hard to explain. Sometimes, no matter how we try to do things right, something still goes wrong. Please be with me in times like that, and help me to see the situation through Your eyes.

Additional Scripture reading: 2 Corinthians 1:3–7

ATTITUDE
CHECK

We do not look at the things which are seen,
but at the things which are not seen. For
the things which are seen are temporary,
but the things which are not seen are eternal.
—2 Corinthians 4:18

Ryan rushed into the waiting room where his mom sat, absorbed in a magazine. She looked up. "Finished already?" she asked.

Ryan shook his head.

Looking at his face, Mrs. Stephens stood up. "Ryan, what is it?"

"I've had an accident," Ryan blurted, expecting to lose his driving privileges for life.

Instead of exploding in anger, his mother threw back her head and laughed. "You've got to be kidding!"

"I'm not, Mom," Ryan said. "The car in front of me rammed me while I was waiting in line."

She laughed harder. Finally, she caught her breath. "I'm sorry, Ryan. But you have to admit, this is sort of funny, that is, unless someone was hurt."

"The officer barely got out of the way," Ryan said, leading his mother toward the accident site.

When Mrs. Stephens saw the damaged cars, she stopped in her tracks. "Betty," she called, "is that you?"

Betty, the woman who had hit Ryan, stepped out of her car. She wiped her eyes with a tissue.

"Jan, is this your car? Oh, I'm so sorry."

Mrs. Stephens surveyed the damage. "Betty, don't worry about it. Our insurance companies will work things out. My car will be fine."

Smiling in relief, Betty said, "I'm glad you aren't upset. I hope my husband is as understanding."

"Oh, if you could have seen Ryan's face just now," Mrs. Stephens said as she tried to suppress a giggle.

Ryan felt his ears burn. *Why does Mom always have to embarrass me?*

Later, after insurance information had been traded and Ryan had passed the test, he drove toward home, a licensed driver.

He said, "Mom, I thought you'd go berserk when you saw the car, but you didn't. How come?"

His mother smiled. "We just got sideswiped by life, that's all. Things like this happen."

"But we're Christians. Shouldn't we be protected from accidents and stuff?"

His mom shook her head. "Not always," she said. "We still live in an imperfect world. Our job is to watch our attitude."

There's that word again, Ryan thought. *Attitude*. "What do you mean?" he questioned.

"Look at it this way. No one was seriously hurt. We both have insurance, and the damage was only minor."

"True."

"Besides, we could be looking at a miracle."

"A miracle?" Ryan asked.

"Well, the Bible teaches that the thief, Satan, comes to kill, steal, and destroy. Maybe, just maybe, Satan planned evil out of this but got whipped."

"Whipped?"

"Yeah, no one was angry. No one was hurt. And for all we know, an angel pushed the officer out of the way just before he would have been crushed."

"Are you serious? An angel?"

"Sure, the Bible tells us unseen battles rage around us. We'll probably never know all the little miracles God performs on our behalf, that is, until we get to heaven."

"I see," Ryan said. "So, before we get upset, we should take an attitude check."

His mom nodded in agreement. "I like how the Amplified

version of the Bible explains it in Philippians 2:5: 'Let this same attitude . . . be in you which was in Christ Jesus.'"

Lord, I give You my attitude. Help me to see things through Your eyes instead of the world's eyes. Let my attitude be in You.

Additional Scripture reading: John 10:7–18

❖

CAUGHT

Grace to you and peace from God the Father
and our Lord Jesus Christ, who gave Himself
for our sins.—Galatians 1:3–4

Ryan had been home for about an hour when the phone rang. It was Jeff Hoffman, the youth director from church.

"Hi, Ryan, it's Jeff."

"What's up?"

"I'm going to be in my office this afternoon, and I wondered if you could drop by. Let's say two o'clock?"

"Sure. I'll try to talk Mom into letting me drive the car."

"You passed your test!"

"Yeah, but it's a long story."

When Ryan arrived at the church, he walked toward Jeff's office, tossing the car keys. *Being able to drive Mom's car feels even better than I expected,* he decided.

Ryan turned toward Jeff's office. He liked talking to Jeff. Jeff made sense.

Welcoming him with a handshake, Jeff motioned for him to sit down. *He's not so bad for a thirty-year-old,* Ryan thought.

"It's been a long time since we've had any time together," Jeff said.

"I've missed it."

"That's one reason why I called you," Jeff explained. "That and the fact I've been putting together a list of names for this year's youth council. Your name's surfaced at the top." Jeff leaned back in his leather chair. "I'd like you to be president."

Ryan dropped his eyes. *I'm not ready for that kind of responsibility,* he thought. *It would be a farce. If only Jeff knew what I'm really like.*

"Sorry, Jeff. No can do."

"Why not?"

The tips of Ryan's ears reddened. "I hate to admit this, but I don't think I'm qualified."

"Qualified?" Jeff asked. "Are you hooked on drugs or something?"

"No," Ryan said, almost laughing. "It's just that I'm not as perfect as everyone thinks." He shifted uneasily. "I'm really kind of a failure when it comes to my walk with Christ."

Jeff stared knowingly as the hair on Ryan's neck began to rise. *Has Jeff guessed my secret?*

Finally, Jeff broke the silence. "Ryan, no one's perfect. We all fall short. So, I'm puzzled. Do you have a problem you need to talk about?"

The blush in Ryan's ears crept into his cheeks. "No, it's nothing."

Leaning across his desk, Jeff said, "No, it isn't nothing. Something is bothering you. Tell me what."

Ryan felt the red creep down his neck. *Should I? Dare I?*

Lord, help me remember nobody's perfect. That, in fact, is why You sent Your Son to die for us, as a sacrifice for our sins. Although I don't want to get entangled in wrongdoing, show me that You continue to forgive me, even when I fail.

Additional Scripture reading: 1 John 2:1–6

❖

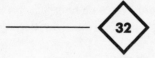

CONFESSION TIME

___

I do not understand what I do. For what I
want to do I do not do, but what I hate I
do. . . . As it is, it is no longer I myself
who do it, but it is sin living in me.
—Romans 7:15, 17 (NIV)

"I really don't want to talk about it," Ryan said, his blush
deepening.

Jeff pressed, "Why not?"

"Just forget it."

Leaning back in his leather chair, Jeff said, "I may have a clue
about what's bothering you."

How can I get out of here? Ryan wondered. His voice shook,
"It's not important."

Looking undaunted, Jeff asked, "Would this have anything to
do with a habit you may have, a habit you use to manage sexual
tension when you're alone?"

Ryan's heart stopped in mid-beat. *Jeff knows!* "Maybe," he
answered, glowing like a rocket's afterburner.

"Well, if that's the case," Jeff said, "you're certainly not alone.
Most guys struggle with this particular problem."

"They do?"

"It causes a lot of embarrassment and self-loathing. Most kids
want to quit but don't know how."

Too embarrassed to speak, Ryan nodded.

"Have you ever wondered what the Bible says about it?"

"What?" Ryan asked.

"It might surprise you, but it says nothing."

"Nothing? But . . . if it's so common, why doesn't the Bible mention it?"

"Maybe because it's not as important as other issues."

Ryan shook his head. "God couldn't approve."

"God created our bodies. He understands our sexuality."

"I hadn't thought of that," Ryan admitted. "But that doesn't make my habit right."

"True, but it may mean God understands, although I'm sure He's saddened when it keeps you from reaching out to Him," Jeff said.

"What do you mean?"

"Well, if you're going around feeling bad about yourself, you might not be able to pray. You might even feel like you have to put God away . . . until you're under control."

"I have been trying to control myself," Ryan confessed. "But I can't."

"Self-control is a worthy goal," Jeff said, "one you should strive toward. But if you fail from time to time, don't be too disappointed with yourself. You might stop and think about what Paul said in the seventh chapter of Romans: 'But what I hate I do. . . . What a wretched man I am! Who will rescue me from this body of death? Thanks be to God—through Jesus Christ our Lord! So then, I myself in my mind am a slave to God's law, but in the sinful nature a slave to the law of sin.'" (NIV)

"Paul makes it sound like doing things you wish you wouldn't do is a common problem," Ryan said.

"Yes," Jeff answered, "it is. That's why you need to be patient and forgiving with yourself."

Ryan sighed. "I'll try."

"Good. I still have a concern, though."

"What?" Ryan asked, still wishing they weren't having this conversation.

"I'm worried about what's going on between your ears."

Narrowing his eyes, Ryan asked, "What do you mean?"

Lord, help me to sort out the difference between true conviction and false guilt. Sometimes, I let guilt get in the way of knowing

You better. Help me to understand my problems, and guide me to the solutions for them. Thanks.

Additional Scripture reading: Romans 7:14–25

❖

THE REAL BATTLE

[We are] casting down arguments and every
high thing that exalts itself against the
knowledge of God, bringing every thought
into captivity to the obedience of
Christ.—2 Corinthians 10:5

Jeff explained, "It's the battle of the mind that is the most dangerous."

"How so?" Ryan asked.

"Well, for example, when you practice your habit, what are you thinking? What pictures are playing in your mind?"

Ryan shrugged.

Pulling a copy of a book off his shelf, Jeff thumbed through its pages. "It's like what Tim Stafford says in his book *Love, Sex & the Whole Person: Everything You Want to Know.* Here it is:

" 'When sexual thoughts come into your mind, it's quite possible to thank God for beautiful girls and for sexuality and just to feel good about being alive as a male in a world full of sexual beauty. You can imagine how wonderful it will be to be married someday. That's good and healthy. . . .

" 'What's not good is to take those thoughts and build on them, manipulate them, obsess yourself with the thought of how much joy you'd get from going to bed with one of those girls.' "

Jeff closed his book. "It's not healthy to look at pornography in your mind or with your eyes," he said.

"Maybe," Jeff continued, "it would be a good idea for you to break some bonds."

"Break bonds?"

"By that I mean you need to verbally renounce any obsessions or porn compulsions and ask God to create a new heart within you. If you work on keeping your heart and mind pure, you'll make progress toward your goal."

Relaxing in his chair, Ryan thought for a moment, then admitted, "This conversation was painful. But I'm kind of glad we had it."

"I am, too," Jeff said as Ryan stood up. "Before you leave, I want to challenge you. Prayerfully consider whether or not you will be the president of the youth council. And try not to carry around so many burdens. Give them to God. Not only does He want your burdens, He wants your heart and soul. He wants to be Lord of your life."

Jeff studied Ryan. "How 'bout some prayer?"

As they bowed their heads, Jeff prayed, "Lord, although Your Word isn't clear on this subject, I sense Ryan is struggling to do what's right. Help him use his struggle as a way to define limits and practice self-control as well as self-forgiveness. Help him realize that we all fail as we struggle to be like You and that You love us regardless.

"Give him purity of mind and heart, and help him not to condemn himself when he fails. Instead, help him use his failures and successes as benchmarks in his effort to grow closer to You."

(To be prayed aloud.) *Lord, I renounce viewing porn, either in my mind or with my eyes. I announce You are in charge of this area of my life. I ask You to direct my eyes and my heart. Please cleanse my mind and set me free.*

Additional Scripture reading: Romans 8:1–4

TOO LATE?

But those who wait on the LORD
Shall renew their strength;
They shall mount up with wings like eagles,
They shall run and not be weary,
They shall walk and not faint.
—Isaiah 40:31

Ryan couldn't believe his eyes. His football was growing larger. He tried to tuck it under his chin. It won't fit. I'll have to climb with one arm!

Crooking the ball in his elbow, he looked up, watching two eagles soar out of sight. If I had wings, I could get to the top of this cliff, no problem, *he thought, staring at the smooth rock above his head.*

Carefully, he began to climb. What's holding me back? *he wondered. He looked down at his throbbing elbow.* It's the football! The tip is jammed in a crack in the rock!

He tugged as hard as he dared, balancing on the ripple of rock beneath his feet while his free hand clutched a tiny ledge above his head. "What am I going to do?" *he asked aloud.*

Again, a gentle breeze wrapped around him. "Trust Me," *a still, small voice seemed to say.*

"God, is that You? What are You trying to tell me?"

"Let go."

Ryan looked down. The space beneath him dropped forever. He squeezed the rock with sweat-slicked fingers. "I . . . I can't, Lord. I'll fall."

He waited, listening for God's voice. The breeze faded, replaced by a song:

Drop your burdens,
Cast your sorrows,
Lay them down at Jesus' feet.
He will lift you,
He will guide you,
Up where eagles glide and sweep.

Ryan opened his eyes. The song on his radio intertwined with his dreams and his thoughts. *If only I could have eagle wings,* he wished. *I'd leave my burdens far behind and soar in the clouds.*

Later that afternoon, he plopped on the couch, planning to watch football. He sighed, *I've got the whole TV to myself. Mom's at the church planning meeting, and who knows where Kristi is.* A line of worry twitched his brow. *She's been avoiding me ever since . . .*

Ryan heard footsteps and turned around in time to spy Kristi ducking out of the room.

"Wait," he called after her.

Kristi stuck her head around the doorjamb. "What do you want?" she croaked.

"Come over here and talk to me," he said.

"I'm too much of a slug," Kristi snapped, walking toward him.

"What?" Ryan asked.

"Those are your words, not mine," Kristi reminded him as she slumped across from him on the recliner.

"I'm sorry I said that," Ryan admitted. "I was angry, and I took it out on you. Can you forgive me?"

Whirling the chair to face the wall, Kristi said, "Your sorry's a little late."

Ryan stood up. "What do you mean?" he asked.

Kristi wrapped herself in the throw quilt and huddled into a ball. "I mean your sorry is as late as my period."

Lord, sometimes I get really tired. Help me to wait on You. As I wait, I will rest, knowing You will lift me up on eagles' wings. I will run and not get weary. I will walk and not faint.

Additional Scripture reading: Psalm 27:1–6

❖

REVELATION

Do not be overcome by evil, but overcome evil
with good.—Romans 12:21

Ryan froze, watching Kristi's shoulders quake.

"Kristi?" he asked. "What are you saying?"

Spinning her chair to face him, she spat out, "What do you care? You've got your own life. I don't seem to be welcome in it."

Ryan stumbled backward as if he'd been slapped. He sat down on the couch, clenching and unclenching his fist. "I'm sorry, Kristi. I didn't mean to hurt you. I've been a real jerk."

"Do you think your little apology's going to make up for what's happened to me?" Kristi asked.

"What *has* happened, Kristi?"

Kristi shuddered, hissing a single word beneath her breath, "Jack."

"Did . . . did he hurt you?" Ryan asked, bolting to his feet again.

Kristi nodded.

Ryan's face paled. He stalked to the window. "I'll kill him, Kristi. I swear it. I'll kill the creep."

"What good will that do?" Kristi asked, twisting a corner of her quilt. "Just because he's ruined my life doesn't mean you should ruin yours."

"Your life isn't ruined," Ryan argued.

"How can I finish high school if I'm going to have a baby? What will my friends say?"

His heart froze. "You mean you're . . ."

"I don't know. All I know is my period is late."

"Does Mom know?"

"What would I say to her? Your perfect daughter, the one who doesn't even have a boyfriend, is pregnant?"

"Kristi?" Ryan hesitated. "I . . . I know you were mad at me that afternoon, but how could you sleep with Jack?"

"I didn't have a choice."

"What do you mean?"

Blowing her nose into a tissue, Kristi said, "He forced me. I tried to fight him off, but he was too strong."

Kristi's shoulders quaked, and Ryan knelt down beside her. She gasped for air. "My life is ruined."

Ryan encircled her in his arms, his shirt damp with her sorrow. "Don't worry, Kristi. I'll think of a way out of this mess."

Kristi wiped her eyes with a tissue and turned her blotchy face to him. "Do you really think you can?"

Ryan nodded, noticing how wounded and frail she looked. "Yeah," he said. "I'll think of something, right after I murder Jack."

Lord, I know the Bible says it's wrong to hate, but some people seem to deserve my hatred anyway. Teach me how to love my enemies, and show me how to forgive those who don't seem to deserve my forgiveness.

Additional Scripture reading: 2 Corinthians 4:7–12

GUILT TRIP

Do you not know that your body is the temple
of the Holy Spirit who is in you, whom you
have from God, and you are not your
own?—1 Corinthians 6:19

Ryan folded his arms under his head and stared at the ceiling of his room. *How could this have happened?* he thought. *What kind of animal is Jack?*

He plumped his pillow and shoved it back into place. *I should have warned Kristi. I should have stopped her from getting into that truck.* He closed his eyes. *Of course, if I hadn't insulted her in the first place,* he thought, *none of this would ever have happened.*

Turning on his side, Ryan stared into the shadows. *Who would have thought Jack wouldn't have understood the word* no?

Ryan remembered Vicki Childs, the girl he had dated last spring.

His cheeks burned. *Maybe we kept our clothes on, but I pushed her, just to see what I could get. I didn't care enough to respect her boundaries.*

Ryan sat up, thumbing through a magazine. A striking girl in an acne medication ad reminded him of Brooke. *I never understood how it felt to be used until Brooke turned the tables on me.*

He sighed. *It hurts to say this, but I don't think she ever cared about me. She wanted a boyfriend who would make her feel important . . . a boyfriend she'd keep any way she could.*

Shaking his head, he thought, *She and Jack should be very happy together.*

The thought of Jack caused Ryan to bolt out of his bed. He faked a punch to the air. "Take that! And that!" he said.

Ryan stopped. *No, a beating would be too good for Jack,* he decided. *I need to think of something worse, something more painful.*

Without warning, Jeff Hoffman's parting words seeped into Ryan's consciousness. "And try not to carry around so many burdens," Jeff had said. "Give them to God. Not only does He want your burdens, He wants your heart and soul. He wants to be Lord of your life."

Ryan walked to his window and looked out over the twilight-shrouded neighborhood. He asked aloud, "Can I give God all of my heart if it's full of hate?"

He turned away. *I can't think about that right now,* he decided. *I've got to think about Kristi. There's got to be a way to get her out of this mess.*

Ryan reached for his phone book and thumbed through the yellow pages. He found the listing: "Abortion Services." Underneath it was an ad for the Summitview Women's Clinic. The words *confidential abortion services* were highlighted in red.

Before Ryan shut the book, he noticed another listing: "Abortion Alternatives." He followed the column with his finger. This listing contained a single entry. He read it aloud, "The Crisis Pregnancy Center." *Which one should I call?* he wondered.

Abortion seems like an awful choice. But it might be the only way Kristi can get out of this mess. Besides, doesn't she have the right to choose?

He closed the phone book. It's an awful choice, a choice he'd make tomorrow.

Lord, teach me to guard my mouth and to respect others. Sometimes, I think only of myself and what's best for me. Help me to remember the other person. Help me to consider not just my friends and family but also the unborn.

Additional Scripture reading: John 8:1–11

RUN-IN

Beloved, do not avenge yourselves, but
rather give place to wrath; for it is written,
"Vengeance is Mine, I will repay," says the
Lord.—Romans 12:19

Ryan slumped on a bench in the sunshine, eating his lunch.

"What's wrong with you?" Shawn asked. "You look terrible."

"I've got a headache," Ryan admitted, slowly chewing his peanut butter sandwich. "I didn't sleep well last night." Ryan took a swig of his cola, then asked, "Shawn, what do you think about abortion?"

Shawn inhaled his pop. "Abortion?" he choked. "Has someone been talking?"

Ryan leaned forward and whispered, "I hope not. Have you heard anything?"

"Uh, no. What could I have heard?"

"Kristi," Ryan admitted with a sigh. "She might need one."

Shawn dropped his jaw. He said, "You're kidding!"

"Jack raped her."

Standing up, Shawn brushed sandwich crumbs off his pants. "She's not preg—"

"I don't know. All I know is, her period's late."

Shawn sat down. "If you're interested in learning about abortion, why don't you call the Crisis Pregnancy Center? They have a lot of information, and they can give Kristi a free pregnancy test."

"What kind of outfit are they?" Ryan asked.

"It's a volunteer group of Christians. They help their clients through crisis pregnancies."

"Do they do abortions?"

"That's not what they're about. But they'd be happy to explain it to you."

"How do you know so much about them?" Ryan asked.

Blushing, Shawn folded his lunch sack. "Oh, I've heard some of the girls talk about it."

Ryan wadded up his paper napkin and started toward a debris-filled trash can outside the shop classroom. Out of the corner of his eye, he saw Brooke wave in his direction. *Whomp!* He smacked into Jack Raymond.

Jack pushed Ryan back. "So, how's the loser today?"

A wave of anger washed over Ryan's body. "What's it to you, imbecile?"

"Imbecile?" Jack asked, pushing Ryan again. "I didn't know you had such a big vocabulary."

Ryan stiffened. "Get out of my way!" he said.

Stepping closer, Jack said, "And I suppose you're going to make me?"

"Ryan!" Shawn warned. "You could get kicked off the team if you hit this creep. He's not worth it."

Deflating like a tired football, Ryan retreated. "You're right."

Ryan started to walk back to the bench when Shawn yelled, "Duck!"

Whirling, Ryan saw Jack swinging a wooden plank he had pulled out of the trash can. He dodged. *Crack!* The plank landed square across his sore shoulder. He thudded to the ground.

Jack tossed the plank back into the trash can. He said, "You're a loser, chump. And from now on, you'd better stay out of my way."

Lord, why are some people's hearts filled with darkness? Send them a light. Show them that no matter how unlovable they seem to be, You created them and love them. You knew them in their mothers' wombs.

Additional Scripture reading: Romans 12:14–21

❖

THE CLINIC

You shall not murder.—Exodus 20:13

Ryan sat out practice on the bench, icing down his sore shoulder. His only consolation was that Jack was sitting out practice, too, on orders from the coach.

"I should suspend you both," the coach had said, "but I'll give you one last chance. Any more fighting and you're off the bench and into the bleachers."

Smiling, Ryan thought, *It might be worth getting kicked off the team to knock Jack off his quarterback high horse.*

Ryan's eyes wandered through the stands and fastened on Kristi. She sat huddled against the cool breeze.

Staring at the ground, Ryan wondered, *Can I really help her fix her problems?*

Afterward, he met Kristi at the family car. He smiled, jingling the car keys.

In silence, he drove Kristi past the Crisis Pregnancy Center to the Summitview Women's Clinic. As they passed the small brick building, Ryan felt a twinge of regret, but he shrugged it off. He was in no mood for fanatics or guilt trips. *We're going to do what's right for Kristi, no matter what,* he decided.

Once inside the clinic, Kristi filled out a number of forms before being ushered away to take a pregnancy test. An hour later, they sat in an office talking to a clinic counselor.

"Honey," Mrs. Grist said, "your test was positive." She breezed ahead, "I've tentatively scheduled your appointment for tomorrow after school."

Mrs. Grist turned and studied Ryan. "Perhaps your friend could drive you home afterward?"

Shrugging a nod, Ryan clenched his fists. *Mrs. Grist is talking like everything's already decided. Isn't she going to explain our options?* he wondered.

Ryan crossed his arms, listening to Mrs. Grist run through her canned speech. *How can it be,* he wondered, *that no one is asking who got this fourteen-year-old girl pregnant?* He narrowed his eyes. *Kristi was raped! Doesn't anyone here care about that?*

As she patted Kristi's arm, Mrs. Grist said, "Honey, choice is your right. All you have to do is sign on the dotted line. We'll take care of the rest."

Ryan frowned. *Maybe this isn't about choice after all,* he decided. *Maybe this is about bucks, big bucks.*

The counselor continued, "Have you decided what arrangements you want to use for payment? We accept both Visa and MasterCard."

Looking at Kristi, Ryan noticed that her eyes were watery and her face blanched white. Squeaking, she asked, "Did you say, I'm pregnant?"

The counselor nodded, oblivious to Kristi's emotional distress. "Yes, we also accept checks or cash."

"Uh, how much does this procedure cost?" Ryan interrupted.

"Four hundred and eighty-five dollars," the counselor responded.

"Kristi, let's go," Ryan said as he stood. "We've got to talk about this."

The counselor stood up, too. "Don't delay too long, or we'll lose our window of opportunity," she warned.

As Kristi and Ryan headed for the door, the counselor called, "Wait a minute." She fumbled for something in her desk drawer. "Here, take these," she said, handing Ryan a batch of condoms. "They might prevent the need for future procedures."

Ryan dropped the condoms onto her desk. "Kristi is my sister," he glowered. "What kind of guy do you think I am?"

The counselor smiled. "It's not my place to judge."

Ryan turned away, hurrying Kristi out of the clinic. When they reached the sidewalk, they were approached by a young blonde woman. "Did you schedule an abortion?" she asked Kristi.

Kristi stared at the ground. "Not yet," she answered, her eyes glistening.

The woman took her hand. "My name is Sara Penrose, and I want to help you. Can we talk?"

Thank You for creating life, even the secret life of unborn children. You knew me even in the womb. Thank You for creating me, and thank You that my mom chose to let me live. Teach me Your way in this issue of life.

Additional Scripture reading: Psalm 139:13–16

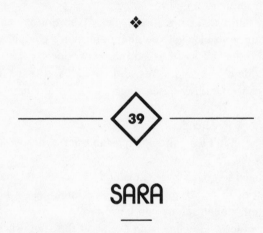

39

SARA

For You formed my inward parts;
You covered me in my mother's womb.
—Psalm 139:13

Ryan, Kristi, and Sara Penrose walked to a nearby park and sat down at a picnic table.

Sara asked Kristi, "Did you get a positive test at the clinic today?"

Nodding, Kristi stared at her hands.

The evening sun glinted on Sara's blonde hair that was pulled back into a ponytail. Her blue eyes softened as she said, "I went through what you're going through about ten years ago. I was about your age when I was raped."

Kristi's eyes snapped to Sara's.

"My attacker happened to be black and everyone, including my social worker, said it would be best for me to abort my child because of her heritage."

Ryan's jaw tensed.

Her eyes glistening, Sara continued, "I tried to convince them that my baby was a person, but they only laughed at me and said I should trust them.

"I remember lying on the abortionist's table," Sara said, "feeling as if I'd been raped again. But that time, I was not only the victim, I was a killer. I had allowed my baby to be pulled, piece by piece, from my womb."

Looking into Kristi's eyes, Sara said, "Abortion is not a quick fix. Did your counselor tell you about abortion's complications?"

"Complications?" Kristi asked, her eyes wide.

Sara nodded. She said, "Yes, did she tell you that sometimes abortions cause sterility, miscarriages, or tubal pregnancies later in life?"

Kristi shook her head.

"I bet she didn't tell you about postabortion syndrome, either."

"What's that?" Ryan asked.

"It's related to grief." Sara explained, "You see, no matter how a mother tries to justify an abortion, she knows she's killed her baby. Her emotional trauma can be severe.

"The people at the clinic won't tell you this, nor will they tell you about the abortion alternative."

"Which is?" Kristi asked, her eyebrows twitching.

"Motherhood," Sara said.

"But," Kristi protested, "I'm too young to be a mother . . . I'm only fourteen."

"Pregnancies last only nine months," Sara reasoned. "And if you want, there are wonderful agencies that could help you place your baby in a loving home, a home you could pick out yourself."

Narrowing his eyes, Ryan asked, "Sara, do you work on commission?"

Sara threw her head back and laughed. "No," she said. "You got my message for free, although the counselor you just left will get fifty dollars if you decide to abort at her clinic."

Ryan turned to Kristi and said, "Perhaps we need to talk with the people at the center."

"Yes," Sara nodded. "And be sure to get another pregnancy test."

"Why?" Ryan asked.

"Lately, it seems the Crisis Pregnancy Center has stopped a lot of girls from getting unnecessary abortions, girls who were never pregnant to begin with."

Lord, it seems that the Establishment is lying to us. It wants us to believe that killing unborn babies is right. It won't let us mention God in the classroom, and it tells us condoms make for safe sex. Lord, help my generation learn the truth.

Additional Scripture reading: Mark 10:13–16

❖

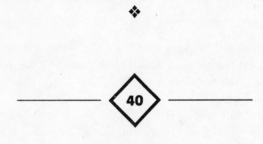

FALSE ALARM

And the Lord will deliver me from every evil
work and preserve me for His heavenly
kingdom.—2 Timothy 4:18

Later that night, Ryan and Kristi sat on the front porch talking in hushed tones.

Ryan said, "It's a relief to know you're not pregnant."

"What I don't understand is how the Women's Clinic could have made such a mistake," Kristi said.

Folding his arms, Ryan said, "Maybe it didn't."

"What do you mean?"

"Maybe the people at the clinic were planning to abort a baby that never existed."

"Why?"

"For the money. Mrs. Grist would have made fifty dollars."

"Could she get away with that?"

"Who's gonna stop her?"

Kristi shuddered. "I'm glad I met Sara today. She saved me from a lifelong guilty conscience."

"Still," Ryan said, "it's scary to think what could have happened. What if the abortionist had botched you up? What if you had gone home and bled to death? Unless I told the authorities what I knew, no one would have suspected the clinic's involvement. Like Sara said, it's almost above the law."

"Well, I'm just glad I'm not pregnant, even though I still feel awful."

"Why?"

Kristi squeezed her eyes tight. "I don't know," she said.

Ryan unfolded his arms and leaned back. "I think you should talk to Mom. Tell her what happened."

"I know I should, but . . ."

"But she can talk to you and take you to our family doctor. With Jack's reputation, I think you should be tested for sexually transmitted diseases."

"You mean like gonorrhea or AIDS?"

Nodding, Ryan said, "Sex isn't safe these days, not even when people use condoms."

Kristi sighed. "Once Mom calms down, she'll know what to do. Maybe she can even help me feel better about myself."

Teach me how to avoid temptation, Lord. Help me respect the girls I date. Teach me to treat them with dignity, honor, and self-control. And if I've already lost my self-control, show me how to regain it. Not just for myself but for my girl and for You.

Additional Scripture reading: James 1:12–16

❖

TEAM THIEF

For the commandments, "You shall not commit adultery," "You shall not murder," "You shall not steal," "You shall not bear false witness," "You shall not covet," and if there is any other commandment, are all summed up in this saying, namely, "You shall love your neighbor as yourself."—Romans 13:9

Shawn asked, "Ryan, have you seen my watch?"

Ryan shook his head. "When did you have it last?" he asked, lacing up his cleats.

"Yesterday, before practice. When I got back to my locker, it was gone. I was hoping it would turn up."

Lowering his voice, Ryan said, "You're not the only team member who's missing something. Ron and Larry lost their wallets last week."

"Great!" Shawn said, slamming his locker shut. "Do you think we have a thief on our team?"

"I hope not," Ryan said with a shrug. "With our big game coming up against Hebert, a petty thief could undermine our morale."

"I just hope our team isn't harboring someone like the Masked Bandit," Shawn joked.

"Very unlikely," Ryan said, grinning. "But speaking of the Masked Bandit, can you believe the nerve of that guy? Two more robberies this week. I'd say he's getting bolder."

"He's stupid," Shawn said. "At the rate he's going, he's bound to get caught. Predictable thieves always do."

"It would be interesting to be there when they finally unmask him, don't you think?" Ryan asked.

"No thanks," Shawn replied. "That guy carries a gun. Besides, I'm more concerned about my watch."

After the warm-up exercises, Ryan faced off against the offensive line. *Will I ever get another chance to win back my quarterback position?* he wondered. *I'm sick of playing defense.*

He quickly bowed his head. *Be with me, Lord. Help me to play my best, even though I'm not where I want to be.*

Opening his eyes, Ryan spied Jack. A flood of anger washed over him. He immediately changed his prayer: *I'm sorry, God, but I'm taking matters back into my own hands. I'm going to use this practice to kill Jack!*

Ryan stomped the ground like a bull. He decided, *That's what practice is for, right? A chance to get even with your enemies, a chance to steal back what's rightfully yours.*

Lord, help me to walk in Your ways. Sometimes it's hard; sometimes it even hurts. But I know I can trust You. For when I do, Your ways become my ways. And when I'm with You, I can find real freedom.

Additional Scripture reading: Ephesians 4:22–32

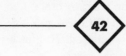

SWEET REVENGE?

Do not rejoice when your enemy falls,
And do not let your heart be glad when he
stumbles.—Proverbs 24:17

At the snap, Jack threw a pitch out to Tom Timmons, the flanker. Ryan whacked through the line, surprising Shawn who had turned to guard Tom. *Crunch!* Ryan knocked Jack flat.

Jack growled, "Have you lost your mind, loser? You're supposed to follow the ball."

Ryan spat on the ground and said, "That one's for Kristi." His eyes sparked hate. "The next one'll be for me."

Clenching his fist, Jack said, "That's right! Be a sucker! I'd like to see you get kicked off this team."

With his heart hammering in his ears, Ryan said, "If I do, I'm taking you out with me."

Again Ryan squatted, head up, eyeing the center. He couldn't look at Shawn. Shawn's eyes would force him to abandon his quest for revenge.

When the ball snapped, Ryan leveled Ron, storming like a Sherman tank. He locked onto Jack, who had already handed off the football. *Who cares?* Ryan decided. *Jack is mine!*

Jack scrambled to sidestep him. *Whap!* Once again, they lay in a snarling heap.

"Get off me, you idiot!" Jack hissed between clenched teeth.

Vaguely, Ryan realized the offense had gained a first down.

It didn't matter until Ryan saw one of the scrubs, Eric Maxwell, trotting his way. Eric pointed at the sidelines. "Coach wants to see you," he said, taking Ryan's place.

Sitting on the bench, Ryan tried to brace himself for Coach's wrath. "We'll talk after practice," Coach growled.

Am I off the team? Ryan wondered. He put his head between his hands and asked, *Lord, now what?*

Deep in the recesses of his mind, he heard a gentle voice answer, "Let go."

Lord, help me to let go of my anger and hatred, even when others seem to deserve my scorn. I give my whole heart to You. Wipe it clean and fill it with Your love. Teach me how to forgive the unforgivable. Teach me how to give up my plans for revenge to You.

Additional Scripture reading: Matthew 5:20–26

43

TRYING TO UNDERSTAND

Do not fret because of evildoers,
Nor be envious of the workers of
iniquity.—Psalm 37:1

"I don't know what happened," Ryan confessed to Jeff Hoffman as they sat together at McGuffy's. "I took one look at Jack, and I snapped."

"Did you get kicked off the team?" Jeff asked.

"No," Ryan said, his eyes wide. "Coach George stuck up for me to Coach Fite. It turns out that Coach George had had a long talk with Shawn. He knows I've been having some personal problems with Jack."

"So are you going to play in Friday night's game against Hebert?" Jeff asked.

"That depends on how I do in practice tomorrow."

Jeff asked, "Are you glad you decked Jack?"

"You know, it didn't do any good. Trying to punish Jack is like trying to punish the ocean. No matter how hard you fight, he keeps coming back in angry waves, trashing anyone who gets in his way. It's like Jack has no conscience or soul."

Jeff raised his eyebrows. "How are you going to deal with him?"

"I don't know," Ryan confessed. "Every time I look at or think about Kristi, I want his blood."

"What would you accomplish if you hurt Jack?"

Ryan shrugged, "I'd feel better."

"But Jack's a guy who doesn't have a chance."

Leaning back in his chair, Ryan asked, "What do you mean? He gets all the breaks. He got my quarterback position, and he got my girl."

"Is he happy?"

"I . . . I don't know."

"Think about it. You said he didn't have a soul. Why is that?"

"How should I know?" Ryan asked, rolling his eyes.

"Let me paint a picture for you. Jack's a guy who's got nothing to live for, except greed and lust. He doesn't know God, and he spends his free time listening to rock music that promotes hopelessness. He's been taught that sex outside marriage is okay. He's got nothing to believe in."

"What are you saying?"

"Today, all of the things that were once considered bad are now considered good. And all of the things that were once considered good are now considered bad."

"Like what?"

"For example, having sex outside marriage, ignoring God, following an alternative life-style, and aborting babies are considered good. On the other hand, praying, witnessing, going to church, saving babies from abortionists, and disagreeing with the sin behind alternative life-styles are considered bad. Don't you see? Everything is turned around. Today, up is down and down is up."

Ryan nodded. "It gets pretty frustrating sometimes," he admitted. "A lot of people think the Christians at school are bigots and snobs. They put us in the same category as racists."

"It's ridiculous," Jeff said. "We Christians are the ones who love our brothers and sisters. There's so much confusion that people like Jack think God doesn't exist. As far as Jack's concerned, life evolved from nothing. Life is nothing. It has no value, no worth."

Ryan wiped his hands on a napkin. "I guess I understand Jack a little better now," he said.

"Do you understand yourself?" Jeff asked.

"What do you mean?"

"Well, you know God. You have hope. You know life has meaning and value. You know the difference between right and wrong. What are you going to do about it?"

"Do?"

"I see you have one of two choices," Jeff said. "Either you can forgive Jack, as God has forgiven you, or you can be consumed with hate. The problem is," Jeff continued, "when you are consumed with hate, you forfeit your relationship with God."

Lord, help me not to fumble the gift of love You've given to me. Instead, help me to pass it to others, including those who seem undeserving. Let my love help guide them into Your end zone. Teach me how to forgive.

Additional Scripture reading: Psalm 37:1–8

RAW FEAR

Strengthen the weak hands,
And make firm the feeble knees.
Say to those who are fearful-hearted,
"Be strong, do not fear!
Behold, your God will come with vengeance. . . .
He will come and save you."—Isaiah 35:3–4

During the pregame warm-ups, Ryan thought through his talk with Jeff. *Jeff helped cool the fire of my hate for Jack,* he realized. *Now, when I tackle Jack in practice, I feel like I'm tackling a dead man, a man without a prayer.*

Ryan dropped to the ground for push-ups. *And what's replaced my hate?* he wondered, sweat trickling off his forehead. He stood up, wiping the dirt off his hands. *Fear,* he admitted to himself.

It's funny, Ryan thought, bending into a stretch, *I don't remember being afraid when I used to play quarterback. That was fun.* He strained to reach his toes. *But now, all I seem to be is a roadblock, a roadblock with too many bruises.*

At the end of the warm-ups, Ryan exchanged high-fives with Shawn, who shouted, "We're going to tear Hebert apart tonight!"

Ryan hesitated a nod. *I hope so,* he thought. *But we haven't started our season with a bang. We're 0–2, plus we haven't beaten our crosstown rivals on their own turf in five years.*

A thunder of cheers went up as the Hebert Panthers ran onto the field. They looked bigger and meaner than they had last year when they had stomped Summitview 27–0.

Ryan's heart skipped a beat as he studied Hebert's quarterback,

Jessy Cramer. Jessy was a two-hundred-pound, six-foot-two senior who could blast the football like a Saturday night special. *Trying to stop Jessy might be like trying to stop a meteorite from blazing across the night sky.*

A few minutes later, the Eagles won the toss. *At least the pressure's off me to start the game,* Ryan thought, dropping onto the bench.

At the end of Summitview's first drive, Ryan cheered when Stan Fredrick caught the ball for a touchdown.

We've got the momentum! he thought, watching the kicker boot the football between the posts.

He trotted to the field to take his position against the Hebert offense. *If only I could regain my hate,* Ryan wished. *At least it would cover up my fear of . . .* He shook his head. *Is it the fear of failure or the fear of injury? Both,* he decided, facing off against the Panthers' center, Bubba Haines.

Haines spit on the ground and growled, "I'm gonna grind your bones into the turf."

Ryan scowled and puffed his lungs full of air, trying to make his slightly thin frame look bigger. He shot off a quick prayer: *Lord, help! Even though I wish I was home in front of my TV, keep me safe and help me play my best.*

Lord, sometimes when I face off against the world, I feel so small. Help me to know You are by my side, directing my path and calling my plays. Teach me how to block the plans of my enemy and how to run with Your love.

Additional Scripture reading: Matthew 10:28–33

CHICKENED OUT

For God has not given us a spirit of fear,
but of power and of love and of a sound
mind.—2 Timothy 1:7

Ryan's defensive game had gone well, despite Bubba's blocks.
And now, with two minutes before halftime, Ryan watched from the sidelines as Jack limped off the field.

Turning to the coach, Ryan caught the nod and trotted to the scrimmage line. *Last week I hoped Jack would break his neck, but now I just feel sorry for him,* he realized, watching the trainer massage Jack's ankle.

Ryan thought, *It's 7–7. A touchdown would sure help things.* He wiped sweat-muddied dirt onto his pants. *But if I blow it,* he decided, *my name will be Mudd . . . Ryan Mudd.*

At the snap, Ryan followed Coach's signals by faking a handoff to his fullback and following Todd James for a gain of five yards before a Panther rolled him to the ground.

Ryan stood up, a little shaky, popping a kink out of his shoulder.

The Eagles huddled again. This time, Ryan called a reverse to flanker Tom Timmons. *We've got to pull it off,* Ryan determined.

When the ball snapped, a Panther linebacker missiled his body toward Ryan. Ryan pushed the football into Tom's numbers, bracing for the impact. *Crunch!* The blow spun him into Tom, knocking the ball free. Todd James captured it beneath his body at the three-yard line.

Ryan's knees wobbled as he pulled himself into a standing position. *I almost blew it!*

He popped his shoulder again. It felt stiff but not too stiff to try a risky blast into the end zone. *This might be a good time to call the kicker for 3. But I've got to do better—I'm going for 6.*

Ryan's heart pounded. "Split left, flanker right—forty-two power pass. Split end post."

As his heart raced into the snap, he thought, *So far so good.* He twisted, pretending to hand off the football to Stan. Stan's flight drew a couple of Hebert Panthers into a chase.

Suddenly, a Panther linebacker broke past Shawn, his breath swirling from flared nostrils. Ryan grimaced, his eyes scanning the end zone. *Where's Larry?*

Ryan stepped back, trying to twist out of the linebacker's path. *I've got to throw now!* he determined. *But where?*

A wave of panic rushed over his body. He closed his eyes and threw deep into the sidelines. *Whack!* The linebacker walloped him to the ground.

I choked. I intentionally grounded the ball! Ryan groaned, smacking the turf.

Ryan shook the stars from his head and staggered to his feet, looking for the ball. His eyes searched the marching band gathered at the sidelines. A squawk from a football-stuffed tuba set off waves of laughter that spread from the band up to the stands.

Oh, great, Ryan groaned to himself. *Why did I chicken? I'll be the laughingstock of the school.*

Lord, help me to let go of my fear and doubt and give them to You. My burdens are too heavy to carry alone. I'd like to exchange my problems and burdens for Your yoke, which is easy and light. Thank You for being willing to help me.

Additional Scripture reading: 1 Peter 5:6–10

ARRESTING FEAR

Cast your burden on the LORD,
And He shall sustain you;
He shall never permit the righteous
to be moved.—Psalm 55:22

The assistant coach, Darrel George, caught Ryan at the door to the locker room. "Step into my office. We need to talk," he said.

As they closed the door, Ryan could hear the muffled thunder of Coach Fite's voice starting his halftime pep talk.

Sitting down across from Coach George, Ryan stared at his dirt-encrusted fingernails.

Coach George broke the silence. "So, Ryan, what's been going on with you?"

Ryan blushed. "What do you mean?" he asked.

"Ever since you came back from your Labor Day weekend, you haven't been yourself."

"My game's off," Ryan said with a shrug.

"Does this have anything to do with your shoulder injury?"

"I don't know."

Coach nodded, leaning back into his chair. "It's obvious. That injury scared you."

Ryan's heart skipped a beat as salty tears stung his eyes. He blinked before Coach George could see them. "I haven't been playing my best," he admitted.

"This isn't the first time I've seen a gifted player choke," Coach George said. "It's a shame. Ryan, I believe you are one of the most talented quarterbacks this team's ever seen."

"Me?" Ryan asked, his jaw dropping.

The coach leaned forward. "Yes. But you're letting your fear manage you. Don't you see? All football players are afraid. The difference is that the others are learning to manage their fear."

"When I saw that Panther linebacker rushing down on me, I panicked. All I could think of was my sore shoulder. My life flashed before my eyes," Ryan said, hanging his head.

"You had good reason to be afraid. But you threw the ball away several seconds before impact. That's not the old Ryan I used to know."

Nodding, Ryan agreed, "I want my confidence back, but I don't know where to find it."

"I'm surprised to hear that," Coach George said. "I know that, like me, you are a Christian. I would think you'd let go of your fear and give it to God."

Ryan's eyes widened as Coach George's words sank in, words that sounded familiar. "Let go?" Ryan questioned.

"Yes," the coach answered. "Let go. Focus on Jesus. Sure, you'll still experience healthy fear from time to time, but Jesus will restore your confidence and help you play your best."

Lord, when I'm captured by my fear, teach me how to turn my eyes from the waves of trouble to Your loving face. Help me to remember that You are always there, ready to take me by the hand if I should fall into a sea of worry or doubt.

Additional Scripture reading: Matthew 11:28–30

SECOND CHANCE

Whenever I am afraid,
I will trust in You.
—Psalm 56:3

The Summitview Eagles jogged into the chill of the night air, their breath swirling before them.

Ryan watched as Jack seated himself on the bench, scowling at an ice pack taped to his ankle.

After the kickoff, the Panthers drove to the twenty-yard line where they were stopped by the Summitview scrub, Eric Maxwell, just short of a touchdown. Ryan cheered, "Way to go, Eric!"

At the turnover, Ryan trotted to the huddle, readying for the snap. He shot off a silent prayer: *Lord, I let go . . . I let go of my hate for Jack. I let go of my fear of injury and failure. I give my efforts to You.*

When Ryan looked up, he caught sight of Jack's glare scouring him from the sidelines. A picture of Kristi's tear-stained face flashed through his mind. *Lord, I hope You don't mind,* he prayed again, *but although I give You my hate for Jack, I don't give him my forgiveness. I can't, Lord. He doesn't deserve it.*

An hour and several touchdowns later, Summitview had the ball on the fifteen-yard line. Ryan looked at the scoreboard and grimaced. *What a time for the coach to leave the call up to me,* he fretted. *With the score 21–17, Hebert's favor, another kick won't do.* He watched the clock tick down to the final forty seconds. *I've got to grab more points.*

As he prepared for the huddle, he prayed, *What should I try, Lord? Another pass play, a ground assault, a sweep? What?* Suddenly, he had an idea.

He called from the huddle, "I right, split left, sixteen draw!"

Adrenaline coursed through his veins at the snap. He stepped back, faking a pass to the right. Right on cue, a Panther linebacker, Butch Holland, burst past Shawn. Ryan's feet danced, pretending a run to the right while he whirled to the left. Butch lunged, grabbing the air as he fell. Ryan spotted the hole where Butch had broken through. Shawn and Todd were fighting to hold it open.

The world tilted into slow motion as Ryan's cleats tore toward the break. His heart pounded in his ears as the roar of the crowd melded with the sound of his breathing. He gained two yards, six yards, eleven yards. The Summitview fans exploded as Ryan stepped over the goal line, raising the football high . . . touchdown!

You are there when I call on You. You hear my cry for help. You take my burdens in exchange for victory. Thank You for providing me Your ear. Thank You for whispering into mine. Thank You for being my Lord.

Additional Scripture reading: Psalm 56:3–11

❖

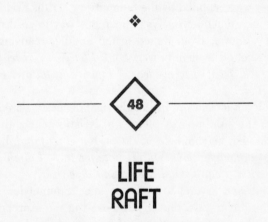

LIFE RAFT

This is My commandment, that you love one another as I have loved you.—John 15:12

Ryan was still stiff when Monday morning arrived. He limped down the school hallway toward his English class where he sagged his body into his seat.

When the bell rang, his teacher, Coach Lovett, looked up from a book. Her crystal earrings glinted in the gleaming morning light.

She flipped her long braid over her shoulder, scanning the classroom with her steely gray eyes. "Today, I have a writing assignment for you."

The class moaned as she continued, "I'm going to describe a situation designed to make you think."

Coach Lovett rose and walked around her desk. She said, "Imagine that a boat is sinking. There is only one life raft for the boat's five passengers. This raft will hold only four people.

"The passenger list includes a pregnant Hispanic woman; a brilliant, though alcoholic, doctor; a childless environmentalist conducting research on the rain forest; a young African-American boy from Chicago; and an older woman who parents a foster baby."

Coach Lovett stated, "Your job is to determine who should live and who should die."

Something triggered in Ryan's half-asleep brain. He tried to resist the impulse but slowly raised his hand.

"Yes, Ryan?"

"What is the purpose of this exercise?"

"It's designed to help you develop your attitudes and judgment," Coach Lovett explained.

"This sounds to me like you are trying to help me develop prejudice."

The class snickered, and Coach Lovett blushed an angry red.

Another student raised his hand. "Ryan's right. This exercise is unfair to minorities."

"And children, older people, singles, alcoholics, and babies," Ryan added.

Flushing, Coach Lovett said, "Very well. The class is free to play the game or write a protest."

Ryan started to smile but caught Coach Lovett's glare. "I'd like to see you after class," she said.

Lord, so many people in our society pretend to teach love but promote hate. Help me to see through their schemes. Help me to value the lives of my brothers and sisters, regardless of their

shape, age, marital status, problems, color, or occupation.
Help me to respect all human life.

Additional Scripture reading: 1 Corinthians 13:1–13

NEW AGE, OLD LIES

In the pride of your heart
you say, "I am a god;
I sit on the throne of a god
in the heart of the seas."
But you are a man and not a god,
though you think you are as wise as a god.
—Ezekiel 28:2 (NIV)

After class, Ryan stood by Coach Lovett's desk while she graded papers. *Help me to speak truth and be bold,* he prayed.

His eyes rested on the book Coach Lovett had been reading earlier, *Teaching the You R Me Concept in the Classroom.*

"What's this book about?"

Coach Lovett smiled up at him. "This book teaches that all people are a single brain cell in a great universal mind."

"Is that what the life raft exercise is about?" Ryan asked.

Coach Lovett hedged, "In part."

"The exercise pointed out our differences. It forced us to play judge, jury, and executioner to whole classes of people," Ryan said.

Smiling patiently, Coach Lovett explained, "I have discovered that death is okay. It's simply a tool that, if needed, can remove cancerous growths from our society."

Ryan's mouth gaped. "Cancerous? You mean people who disagree with your ideas are cancerous?"

She laughed. "The way you put it makes the New Age movement sound evil. It's really a beautiful thing. When you discover that you are a god, your whole sense of reality changes."

Shaking his head, Ryan said, "I don't believe we can be gods."

"Then you've limited your thinking," Coach Lovett said.

Ryan countered, "We studied this in youth group at church. You see, I believe in the one God of the Bible. I also believe in the *original sin*."

"The original sin?"

"Well, if you remember the story of the Garden of Eden, you might recall that Eve wanted to *be like God*. That's why she ate the forbidden fruit."

"Maybe you need to taste the fruit of a new way of thinking," Coach Lovett charged. "You'll discover that the Bible is only one of many paths to God."

"The Bible teaches that Jesus is the only way," Ryan explained.

"That idea is bigoted," Coach Lovett responded.

"Bigoted? But Christ taught us to love our neighbors and our enemies. He lifted the value of all people."

Coach Lovett rose from her desk. "I see that talking to you about the enlightenment is a waste of time. I've got to get ready for my next class," she said.

As Ryan walked toward his locker, he thought, *I hope Coach Lovett is open-minded enough not to flunk me for disagreeing with her. I've got to keep my grades up for the big game against Bingman High.*

O God, who created the universe, help me not to be seduced into believing that I am You. Thank You for creating my mind and giving me the choice to worship You.

Additional Scripture reading: Genesis 3:1–19

❖

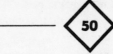

THE CONFESSION

O God, You know my
foolishness;
And my sins are not hidden from
You.—Psalm 69:5

After Monday's practice, Ryan joined Shawn on the bench as the other players hustled into the locker room. "You looked great playing quarterback this afternoon," Shawn said.

Ryan stared across the field. "Thanks," he said. "But we'll see what Jack has to say about it when his ankle heals."

Following Ryan's gaze, Shawn commented, "She's pretty all right."

Ryan blushed. "Who?" he asked.

"That blonde trying out for cheerleader. The one who comes to youth group sometimes. What's her name?"

"Jenni," Ryan replied, grinning shyly. "Jenni Baker."

"I think she'd make a great cheerleader," Shawn observed.

Nodding, Ryan said, "She's definitely the best prospect. But I'm confused. Why are they having cheerleading tryouts now, four weeks into the season? Does Jackie know what's going on?"

"Jackie resigned," Shawn said, kicking at a rock.

Ryan knitted his brows together. "Resigned? I thought she loved the squad."

"She does."

Blinking hard, Ryan studied his friend. "Does this have anything to do with why you didn't suit up today?"

Shawn ducked his head. "Yes."

"What's going on? Is everything okay?"

"Well, I guess I'm kind of surprised you haven't heard something before now."

"Heard what?"

"Jackie's pregnant."

"What?" Ryan dropped his helmet and fumbled to pick it up. "That can't be right. You and she would never . . ."

"We never intended to," Shawn admitted. "But things got hot between us. We couldn't handle it. We blew it big time."

"Why?" Ryan asked. "You're a strong Christian. How could this have happened?"

"We dropped our guard," Shawn said. "We made mistakes that caused our relationship to get too steamy."

"What do you mean?"

"First off, we should never have kissed in reclining positions. Jackie tried to say no, but I insisted. I thought it was innocent fun.

"My second mistake was slipping my hands under Jackie's clothes. She resisted that, too, but I eventually got my way."

Ryan stared at Shawn, too shocked to interrupt.

"The third mistake I made was to listen to sexy music and to take Jackie to passionate movies. Later, when we were alone, I couldn't get those sexy Hollywood scenes out of my mind. I got to where I was so hot and bothered I couldn't think straight.

"I began to pressure Jackie, to wear down her arguments. One night, she gave in.

"We used condoms, but one of them must have failed because now . . . now we're going to have a baby."

Ryan's head spun from Shawn's confession. "Wow," he said, "I can't believe this has happened."

Lord, help me not to take the path that leads, one step at a time, to sexual sin. Teach me how to guard my mind and respect my girlfriend. I dedicate all relationships that may come my way to You. Help me to avoid temptation and stay true to my commitment to You.

Additional Scripture reading: Psalm 119:101–117.

❖

FATHERHOOD

———

And you shall do what is right and good in the sight of the LORD, *that it may be well with you.*
—Deuteronomy 6:18

"So what are you going to do?" Ryan asked.

Shawn answered, "I'm dropping off the football team so I can get a job after school."

"You're dropping off the team?"

"Jackie's parents have three other children at home, and there's not a lot of money for extras. Now, with the baby coming, there are going to be more expenses and doctor bills. I'm going to do what I can to help out."

"But you're our right guard. How are we going to replace you?"

"The coaches and I planned ahead. That's why a couple of the scrubs are still hanging around."

"You told the coaches, but you didn't tell me?"

"I'm sorry," Shawn said. "I didn't want to hurt you. For a while, I thought the problem might go away."

"Go away?"

"At first, Jackie considered having an abortion. But after talking to the people at the Crisis Pregnancy Center, we decided that Jackie should carry our baby to term."

"I admire you two for that."

"It wasn't the easiest decision," Shawn admitted.

Ryan asked, "So, are you getting married?"

Shawn shook his head. "No," he said. "We both agreed we're too young for that. We want to go to college someday. A baby now would change our future."

"Your future, you mean. What's Jackie going to do? Raise the baby alone?"

"No," Shawn said. "We've started talking to a Christian adoption agency. We've been thumbing through their portfolios, and we've discovered some really neat Christian couples out there who'd make wonderful parents for our baby."

"Still, I can't believe that you're really going to be a father," Ryan commented.

"Neither can I," Shawn said with a sigh.

Ryan put his arm around Shawn's shoulder. "You're doing the right thing. Your decision saved a life."

Leaning back, Shawn smiled at a passing cloud. "Yeah, who knows?" he said. "Maybe someday, my kid will be at this very high school, on this very football field. I may not be in the stands cheering for him, but I'll be smiling just the same, smiling in my heart."

Lord, teach me how to be responsible for my actions, regardless of the cost. Help me not to take the easy way out, but show me how to follow You when the going gets tough. Help me do the right thing.

Additional Scripture reading: Matthew 5:13–16

❖

TO CATCH A THIEF

The accomplice of a thief is his own enemy;
he is put under oath and dare not testify.
—Proverbs 29:24 (NIV)

After Shawn left, Ryan sat on the bench, watching Jenni practice her cheers. Finally, a brunette nudged Jenni and pointed at him.

Ryan grinned and Jenni blushed. *She's cute, all right,* Ryan decided, standing up to stretch. *I'll have to call her sometime . . . sometime soon. Homecoming's just around the corner.*

As Ryan entered the deserted locker room, he listened to the stillness. His head snapped toward a clicking sound coming from Coach George's office. *Is Coach George still here?* he wondered. He moved closer. *No, the lights are off.*

Tiptoeing quietly, he crept forward. *Why is his door cracked open? Coach George always locks it before he leaves for the day.*

Ryan eased up to the door and pushed. *Snap!* He heard a noise behind Coach George's desk.

"Hello?" he called. "Is somebody there?"

Eric Maxwell's head popped up.

"Oh, it's you," Ryan said. "What are you doing?"

Blushing, Eric answered, "Uh, I left my English book. I came back to get it."

Ryan stepped toward him and asked, "You left your English book behind Coach George's desk?"

Eric nodded.

"Then," Ryan asked, leaning forward, "what are you doing with the team's cash box?"

Trembling, Eric slumped into Coach George's chair. "You caught me," he said.

Ryan's eyebrows arched. "You . . . the team scrub . . . you're the team thief?" he asked. "Why?"

"I need coke."

"Coke?"

"You know, snow, powder, the white stuff."

"You mean cocaine?" Ryan asked, his eyes squeezed into narrow slits.

"Yeah," Eric admitted, staring at the cement floor.

"Don't you know that junk will kill you?" Ryan asked.

"I've been using it only a few weeks."

"It's *addictive,* man!"

"I didn't think one little sniff would hurt me," Eric said. "Some guy gave me a free sample at Todd's party. The next thing I knew, I wanted more and more."

Ryan pulled up a chair, blocking Eric's escape route. "Eric," he said, "I think we need to talk."

"Are you going to nark on me?" Eric asked.

"What do you think? Drugs and stealing are serious problems . . . problems that will destroy your life. What do you want me to do, sit back and watch you throw everything away?"

Eric pleaded, "Let me go. I promise I'll straighten up."

Ryan said, "I can't do that. I don't turn my back on my friends when they need my help."

Lord, help me not to become dependent on anything or anyone but You. If someone should offer me a high, help me see it as a trap—a trap that will steal my mind and body. Give me the courage to say no. Thank You.

Additional Scripture reading: Luke 4:17–21

❖

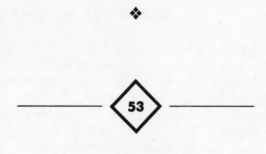

HOOKED

Surely He shall deliver you from the snare
    of the fowler
And from the perilous pestilence.
    —Psalm 91:3

"Are you going to call the police?" Eric asked as Ryan reached for the phone.

"No," Ryan said, "I'm calling Coach George. This is his office. He'll know what to do with you."

Ryan dialed the number. He said, "Hello, Coach George, this is Ryan. Listen, there's a situation here. I think you need to come back down to the gym. I'm here with Eric Maxwell . . . uh huh . . . he's in trouble, serious trouble."

Hanging up the phone, Ryan looked at Eric, who had melted into the chair. "He's on his way," Ryan said, staring at the freshman.

"Why did you go and do that?" Eric stammered, the tip of his nose turning red. "Don't you know what will happen? Coach George will kick me off the team."

"Coach will do whatever he thinks will help you."

Eric clenched his fist and shouted, "I don't need his help. I NEED MY DRUGS!"

"Why?" Ryan asked.

"I've always been a nobody," Eric confessed. His voice shook, "I'm an empty shell with eyes. Coke put something inside me. It killed my pain."

"You want to destroy your life and walk around in a zoned-out cloud?"

Eric shrugged, "What else is there?"

"Have you ever thought about turning to God?"

"God? Didn't you know? He's been kicked out of our society. You can't find Him anywhere anymore."

"I think I'm beginning to understand why your life feels empty," Ryan said.

"What makes you an expert?" Eric challenged.

"When I was twelve, my dad left home," Ryan said. "I was totally lost without him. I prayed and asked God to bring him back, but He didn't. At first, I didn't want anything to do with God."

"What made you change your mind?"

"I was at summer camp a couple of years ago with the kids from church. I began to realize how empty I was. That's when I decided to try God. I asked Him to come into my life and to forgive me of my sins."

"What happened?"

"Nothing much at first," Ryan admitted. "My change was gradual. Over time, I began to feel God's love, and I realized I wasn't empty anymore. One day, I discovered God had become a part of my life—a Friend who would hear my prayer, a Father who would guide me, and a God who loved me enough to send His Son to die for me."

"I wish I could experience that," Eric admitted.

"You can," Ryan said.

"How?"

"It's a process."

"How do you start?"

"First, you need to invite God into your life. Then you need to accept the forgiveness He offers you through His Son, Jesus Christ."

"That guy who died on the cross?"

Ryan nodded. "Yeah. Then you need to make Him Lord of your life."

"How?"

"Give your problems to God."

"What good will that do?"

"God may not poof your problems out of existence, but He will shoulder them for you."

"Is that all there is to it?"

"I'm beginning to discover something new. I can listen to God's Holy Spirit. I can hear His voice. It happens in different ways . . . through Christian music and Scripture . . . and sometimes when I'm quiet, He speaks softly to my heart. It's really awesome. It's like my adventure with Him has just started," Ryan said.

Come into my life, Lord, and forgive me of my sins. Help me to let go of my problems and give them to You. I give You control of my life. Please be my Lord, my Friend, and my God.

Additional Scripture reading: 1 John 2:15–17

WRONG NUMBER?

Show me Your ways, O LORD;
Teach me Your paths.—Psalm
25:4

Ryan paced in his room, trying to get up his nerve to call Jenni Baker. *This would be the perfect time,* he realized. *With Mom and Kristi at the doctor's, I've got the house and phone all to myself.*

But what will I say to her? he wondered. *What if she doesn't even know who I am? Should I remind her?* He practiced into his mirror, "Hi, this is Ryan Stephens, the tuba-slugging football player."

He grimaced. *No, I need something better.* He looked into the mirror again. "Hi, this is Ryan Stephens from church . . ."

Shaking his head, he sat down on his bed. *What's the use?* he wondered. *The way everything's turned out, maybe I should avoid girls altogether.*

He flopped back on his bed. *No, that's impossible,* he decided, staring at the ceiling.

He stared at the round light fixture overhead. *But what can I do to prevent the mistakes Shawn made with Jackie? Maybe,* he decided, *Jenni and I could go out with other kids on group dates. And maybe we could go to youth group or dinner at McGuffy's. But whatever we do, reclining and frisking in the back seat of Mom's car are out,* he resolved.

Sitting up, Ryan tried to summon his courage. He couldn't. *What was it Coach George said?*

"All football players are afraid. The difference is that the others are learning to manage their fear."

All right, he decided, *I'll do it scared. And I'll do it before Kristi and Mom walk through the front door.*

He looked up Jenni's number and dialed the phone. A feminine voice answered, "Hello?"

"Hi," Ryan said, his words tumbling out, "this is Ryan Stephens. I know you from church. Uh, listen, I was wondering if you'd like to go to youth group with me Saturday night. Maybe we could end up at McGuffy's for a hamburger or something."

Ryan paused to catch his breath. His ears met silence.

"I can't," the voice finally answered. "My husband doesn't allow me to date . . . but maybe you would like to talk to my daughter, Jenni. She might be available."

Closing his eyes, Ryan could feel the tips of his ears prickle with heat. "Oh . . . uh . . . is she there?" he stammered.

"I'll get her."

Ryan slumped against the wall and rolled his eyes. He shot off a quick prayer: *Lord, I'm sorry. I forgot to include You in this adventure. Would You please make this phone call all right? And if it's okay, could Jenni please say yes?*

Soon he heard giggles approaching the other end of the phone. "Hi, this is Jenni."

"Uh, hi. This is Ryan Stephens."

"I know. Mom told me."

Ryan's prickles spread to his cheeks. "Listen, I was wondering if you'd like to go out with me Saturday night. I thought that maybe we could go to youth group, then grab a hamburger afterward . . ."

"I'd love to," Jenni said.

Thank You, Lord, that I can call on You any time of the day or night and You will hear me and help me. Lead me in Your path, and let my ways be Your ways. Help me to do what's right, even if I have to do it scared.

Additional Scripture reading: Psalm 25:1–11

❖

CONFIDENCE FOUND

It is better to trust in the LORD
Than to put confidence in man.
—Psalm 118:8

Power surged through Ryan's veins as he blasted the football to Stan Fredrick for a first down. He sneaked a peek at Jack who was still benched with his ankle injury.

Frowning, Ryan thought, *Maybe, with my rival out of practice, I'm experiencing a little false confidence.*

Ryan called the play from the huddle, "Split right, flanker right. Ten sprint. Pass on the first hut!"

He took his position and readied his stance. *Maybe so, but my new confidence also has something to do with the fact that I'm finally figuring out my relationship with God. I'm finally learning how to listen to His voice and to give up my hatred for Jack.*

"Green forty-two. Green forty-two. Go, set, hut!"

Falling back, Ryan faked a handoff to Stan. He ran to the right, looking deep for Larry. *He's there!* Ryan blasted the football through the air. *Another first down!*

Ryan turned to exchange high-fives with Shawn, but all he found was a grinning scrub.

A pang of sadness gripped him. *I miss not seeing Shawn around. I miss not having a Christian friend on the team.*

Shawn wasn't the only one who was missing; so was Eric. Eric had gone into a private drug rehab center. *But now he's beginning to get to know Jesus,* Ryan thought. *Things may be hard for him, but I have a feeling he's going to be okay.*

He looked at the new lineman, Tyrone Winner, a big sophomore the coaches had pulled from junior varsity. *Things look good,* Ryan decided. *But what will happen when Jack's on his feet? Will things go back the way they were, or will I get to stay on as quarterback?*

Ryan sighed and trotted to the huddle. *Well, I'm not going to worry about it,* he decided. *I'm going to turn the whole thing over to the Lord. It's His problem now, not mine. All I have to do is to play my best and have a little fun. That's what football's supposed to be all about, right?*

The ball snapped, and Ryan was ready with a ground assault. His cleats threw sod into the air as he faked to his right, twisting around a defensive tackle.

Crunch! He was hit from the side. The new JV recruit helped him to his feet. "Not bad, Tyrone," Ryan said, patting his back. "You may have a place on this team."

Tyrone grinned. "Man, I'm counting on it."

Ryan stole a glance at Jack and looked back at Tyrone. "Nothing would please me more."

Sometimes a little time has to pass before I can see how involved You are with my life. I will never know how many times You intervene for me. I thank You for that. Help me continue to grow in You, and help me continue to give my burdens to You.

Additional Scripture reading: Psalm 118:5–9

THE
JOKER

And be kind to one another, tenderhearted,
forgiving one another, just as God in Christ
also forgave you.—Ephesians 4:32

Ryan sprinted to the locker room feeling tired but happy. Coach
Fite stopped him. "Looked good out there, Stephens."

Ryan's grin was stopped short by Jack's glare. He turned to the
coach. "Thanks, I think my game's back."

Trotting ahead, Ryan reflected, *I wonder if Coach Fite will
reinstate me as quarterback?* Holding his head a little higher, he
thought, *I hope so. But I've got a lot of work to do before the big
Homecoming game against MacArthur. They're 3–0, rated number
one in our conference.*

Pulling off his damp things, Ryan caught a whiff of his jersey.
*I really need to clean this thing, but I hate to wash all the personality
out of it.*

He grabbed his towel and headed for the showers.

Ryan stepped under a jet of water, while the guys held their
noses. Stan called, "Phew! Ryan, ever think of trying a little de-
odorant before practice?"

"My scent is my secret weapon," Ryan said with a laugh.

"It's not so secret," Stan shot back, throwing Ryan a bar of
soap.

As the warm water pelted Ryan's face, his friends headed back
to the locker room, popping each other in a towel-fighting frenzy.
Click!

What was that? Ryan asked himself, wiping the suds out of his
eyes. *It sounded like the shower room door.*

He turned the water off and treaded to the exit. *It's locked!*

He looked up just in time to catch a glimpse of Jack's grinning face through the small glass window.

Ryan pounded on the door and yelled. "Hey, somebody, let me out!"

The howling game of towel chase continued. *They can't hear me!*

Ryan looked at the connecting locker room door and sighed in relief. *It's open.*

His feet splashed to the entrance of the junior varsity dressing room.

He pulled his towel around him and looked about. The place was deserted. *Great,* he thought. *Maybe I'll get out of here after all. All I have to do is sneak through the gym and back around before anyone catches me!*

Just as he was halfway to his goal, the gym door burst open and the cheerleaders scampered in.

Oops, there's Jenni! Ryan realized, sliding on his wet feet.

Turning toward his sprinting figure, the girls squealed into giggles. Ryan ran faster, almost slipping past the locker room entrance.

He ducked but not before he caught a glimpse of Jenni's blush.

Ryan frowned as his ears tingled. *What will Jenni think of me now?*

He shook his head. *Jack's a jerk!* he thought. *I hate him! Is there no end to his torment?*

As he rounded the corner, Jack guffawed with laughter. "It's the school flasher!" he taunted. "Wait till the cheerleaders spread this around. Everyone will be laughing at ya, Tuba Man."

Lord, You said that if I didn't forgive others for their wrongs against me, You wouldn't forgive me for my wrongs against You. But sometimes, it's so hard. I don't have enough love within myself to forgive some people. Lord, please give me Your power and love to forgive others. Thanks.

Additional Scripture reading: Hebrews 12:1–2

❖

HOLDING ON

If someone says, "I love God," and hates his
brother, he is a liar; for he who does not love
his brother whom he has seen, how can he love
God whom he has not seen?—1 John 4:20

Ryan lay down on his bed and thought about his day.

He'd had a good football practice, and Coach Lovett had signed
his eligibility slip for Friday night's game.

As he turned to set his alarm clock, he smiled at Kristi's news.
Although her AIDS test hadn't come back yet, her other STD tests
were negative.

*The news was hard on Mom, but I'm glad we told her. I hated
to see Kristi trying to deal with this alone. Mom'll make sure she
gets help. She's even trying to talk Kristi into going to the police.*

Pulling the covers to his chin, Ryan decided, *I'll never forgive
Jack for what he's done to my family and me. Never. Besides, God
wouldn't expect me to.*

He shut his eyes, and the sounds of Jack's taunts began to play
through his mind.

*As Jack jeered, Ryan felt a heavy weight clamp around him.
What's this? he wondered.*

*Ryan looked down the mountainside and realized he and Jack
were linked together by a rope. His eyes bugged. We're on belay!*

*With sweaty hands, Ryan clung to an overhanging rock while
Jack's body dangled from the end of his rope. How much longer
can I hang on? Ryan questioned as Jack swung in the breeze.*

*"What's the matter?" Jack called from below. "Can't you get a
grip?"*

"Shut up!" Ryan yelled.

Jack screamed back, "What do you think you're doing? Are you going to lug me everywhere you go?"

Jack's nothing but a dead weight. A weight that'll pull me down, Ryan thought before shouting, "If I let go, you'll fall."

"That's where you're wrong," Jack bellowed. "If you let go, we'll fly."

Jack pointed to a gliding eagle. His voice echoed, "See? We'll fly . . . fly . . . fly."

Ryan gripped the rock tighter, and a breeze stirred around him. Is that You, Lord? Ryan prayed.

A gentle voice answered, "Trust Me. Cut your rope and follow Me."

Ryan shook his head. "I can't, Lord. There's got to be another way . . . a way that makes more sense."

By not forgiving others, I carry around a dead weight everywhere I go. It's a weight that will stop me from knowing You. Help me cut the chains that bind and learn how to free myself in Your love.

Additional Scripture reading: 1 John 4:15–21

SURPRISE WITNESS

A man who has friends must himself be
friendly,
But there is a friend who sticks closer
than a brother.—Proverbs 18:24

Ryan took a deep breath and opened the car door. *I'll probably have to face Mrs. Baker,* he realized, walking to Jenni's door. *She probably thinks I'm an idiot, especially if she's heard about the shower incident. Maybe she won't even let Jenni go out with me!*

He wiped his sweaty hands on his pants and rang the doorbell.

Mrs. Baker swung open the door. She said, "You must be Ryan."

The tips of Ryan's ears burned. He said, "Nice to meet you."

Mr. Baker appeared at the door. "I've heard a lot about you," he said.

Ryan's voice rose an octave. "You have?"

"Yes. I hear you're the starting quarterback on the football team."

Relaxing, Ryan replied, "At least in our game against Bingman last night."

"That was a great win!" Mrs. Baker said. "How many of the touchdown passes did you throw?"

"Three," Ryan admitted.

"And he even ran one in himself," Jenni said with admiration.

Ryan turned to see Jenni standing at the foot of the stairs. Her soft curls framed her deep blue eyes, and her face reflected the warmth of her peach sweater.

Ryan's breath caught in his throat. "Hi. You look really nice tonight."

"Thanks."

Turning to Mr. Baker, Ryan asked, "When should I have Jenni back?"

"We have church in the morning. How about eleven?"

"Fine," Ryan said.

As they walked to the car, Ryan thought, *I really don't know anything about Jenni, other than she made the cheerleading squad and goes to youth group. What should I say to her?*

He opened the car door for her. *Maybe,* he mused, *I can ask her a few questions about herself and try to find out what makes her tick.*

Their first few moments alone were awkward before Ryan asked, "So, how do you like being a cheerleader?"

Jenni laughed, "I'm not sure yet. This is something my friend, Kara Daniels, talked me into. Coach Lovett says she wants me to start cheering with the squad next week."

"Good old Lovett," Ryan said with a smile. "I'm glad she signed my eligibility slip for last night's game. I wasn't sure if she would."

"I admire you for standing up to her in class the other day," Jenni said.

"I was afraid it was a dumb move. Coach Lovett could have finished my career with the football team."

Jenni confessed, "I was afraid she'd can me from the cheerleading squad when she read my essay."

"You mean you backed me up?"

Nodding, Jenni answered, "That life raft game is an exercise in prejudice. I hate prejudice."

Ryan studied Jenni with new admiration. "Really!" he said. "So do I."

Lord, teach me how to be a friend to others. Help me not to focus only on myself and my needs, but help me to focus on the needs of others. Teach me how to listen and how to care.

Additional Scripture reading: 2 Corinthians 6:14–18

TODD'S DECISION

—

I am the door. If anyone enters by Me, he will be saved, and will go in and out and find pasture.—John 10:9

Ryan was surprised to see Todd James at the youth group meeting. *What's he doing here?* he wondered. *I thought he was a party guy.*

Leaning toward Jenni's ear, Ryan whispered, "Isn't that your friend, Kara Daniels, with Todd?"

Jenni nodded as Pastor Jeff began his talk to the crowd of about forty teenagers. Jeff said, "My topic tonight is God's love. How many of you believe God really loves you?"

A shy wave of hands rippled the air. "Good," Jeff announced. "How many of you deserve that love?"

When no hands were raised, Jeff continued, "Tonight, I want to tell you a story Jesus once told. . . . A certain man had two sons. They all worked hard on their family farm. But the younger son secretly plotted to leave. *After all,* he reasoned, *anything's gotta be better than a life of farm work.*

"One day, he approached his father. 'Dad, I've helped you build this farm, and now I'm ready to cash in, pick up my half of the inheritance, and travel to the big city to make my own way.'

"Reluctantly, the father mortgaged the family farm and gave his son his half of the money. The next day, the son packed his bags and left for adventure in the big city.

"At first, life seemed good to the young man. He had money, friends, and parties. That is, until his inheritance ran out. Deserted by his friends, he set out looking for work, but work was hard to come by.

"Finally, the young man found a job feeding hogs. He was so hungry he almost ate the hog swill.

"One day, as he walked through the muck of the hog yard, he thought, *Even my father's hired workers have food to spare, and here I am starving to death. I will go home. I'll say, 'Dad, I've sinned against you and heaven. I am no longer worthy of being called your son. Make me one of your hired servants.'*

"Back home, the father kept a watchful eye on the road, always hoping for some word from his son. This day, as he turned to study the road, he saw a figure in the distance. It was his lost son! The farmer's heart was filled with compassion, and he ran to embrace his boy."

Jeff continued, "Let me read the rest of the story in the words of Jesus, found in Luke, the fifteenth chapter. The boy said, 'Father, I have sinned against heaven and in your sight, and am no longer worthy to be called your son.'

"But the father said to his servants, 'Bring out the best robe and put it on him, and put a ring on his hand and sandals on his feet. And bring the fatted calf here and kill it, and let us eat and be merry; for this my son was dead and is alive again; he was lost and is found.' "

Jeff looked up. "There is probably someone here tonight who is in a far country. You are away from your Father God, who loves you."

Ryan glanced at Todd. *He's listening!*

"Maybe you don't care," Jeff said. "Your parties are too much fun. But be sure of this, life will catch up with you. Your bills will come due. Don't wait until that day.

"Turn your eyes toward home. God is waiting for you."

Todd shifted uneasily in his chair.

"God loves us so much He sent His Son, Jesus, whose death and resurrection created a door that joins God and us."

Jeff searched the crowd and his eyes rested on Todd. "Through Jesus, we can come home to God. Then, God can see us as whole, forgiven, and pure, no matter what we've done in the big city.

"Why die of starvation? Why not come home?"

I don't want to be on the run from Your love. Instead, give me the courage to enter the door You have provided me so I can

*participate in the plans You have for my life. And if I have
strayed, lead me to the path that will take me back to You.*

Additional Scripture reading: Psalm 119:29–37

❖

A ROTTEN WITNESS

Two are better than one,
Because they have a good reward for their labor.
For if they fall, one will lift up his companion.
But woe to him who is alone when he falls,
For he has no one to help him up.
   —Ecclesiastes 4:9–10

After Jeff's talk, the teens milled around the room.

"How about a breath of fresh air?" Ryan asked Jenni.

Jenni nodded and they headed outside, hand in hand.

When Ryan swung open the front door of the church, he froze
in his tracks. Kara, Todd, and Jeff Hoffman were praying in the
church parking lot.

Ryan and Jenni approached cautiously. Todd was whispering a
prayer: "God, it's me. You know who I am. You know the things
I've done. Please forgive me. I give my life to You."

Ryan and Jenni crept closer.

"Something's happening," Todd said, looking up. "It's like I'm
being made brand-new!"

"That's a good way to put it, Todd," Jeff said. "You've just been born again. God is imparting His Holy Spirit into your life."

Todd laughed. "This feels great," he said. "Why didn't you tell me this would happen? I'd have become a Christian years ago."

Turning, Todd saw Ryan and gave him a high-five. "Ryan? Are you a Christian, too?"

Ryan nodded.

"Why didn't you tell me?" Todd asked.

A wave of shame engulfed Ryan. "You didn't know?"

Todd shook his head. "I never would have given you those whiskeys at my party," he said.

Jeff cocked his head. "Whiskeys?" he asked.

"And I never should have drunk 'em," Ryan answered.

Disappointment shot across Jeff's face. He turned to Ryan. "You got drunk?" he asked.

Jenni stared as Ryan threw his hands up in the air. "I wasn't thinking," he said. "But don't worry. Most of the booze ended up on my mom's new carpet. I learned my lesson. Not only was I poisoning my body, I was killing my witness."

Turning to Todd, Ryan said, "I'm sorry. I never knew until this moment how dumb that stunt really was."

"We've all got a lot to learn," Todd responded.

Ryan nodded. "It'll be good to have another Christian friend."

"Yeah," Todd agreed. "We'll learn together."

"You got it!" Ryan said with a grin.

Lord, the way I handle life is even more important than I thought. Others are watching. They are wondering about my hope and faith in You. Give me the courage to take a stand and to be a witness for You.

Additional Scripture reading: Acts 22:14–16

THE
MOVIES

—

> The lamp of the body is the eye. If therefore
> your eye is good, your whole body will be full
> of light. But if your eye is bad, your whole
> body will be full of darkness. . . . How great
> is that darkness!—Matthew 6:22–23

Later, at McGuffy's, Ryan spotted a couple from youth group sitting at a booth.

Dee Ann Miller called to him and Jenni, "Come and join us!"

As they sat down, Dee Ann said, "I think I've got Matt talked into taking me to see *Gross Night of the Bloody Knife!* Do you and Jenni want to come?"

Ryan turned to Matt Daniels, "What's the movie about?"

Matt shrugged, "I think it's some kind of horror movie spoof."

"Brooke told me it was hysterical," Dee Ann said. "Come on. It'll be fun."

Twenty minutes later, Ryan stood in line for the movie.

What am I doing? he wondered. *This might be one of those steamy movies Shawn warned me about.*

Looking up, Ryan studied Todd and Kara, who had joined them. *Here I go ruining my witness again.* He sighed. *At least the movie gets out before eleven o'clock, in time to make Jenni's curfew.*

The movie started with a heavy love scene. Ryan could feel his ears burn. *This is a lot of sexual pressure. I can't believe Jenni and I are watching this.*

Later, when a gore-encrusted phantom thrust his blood-stained knife into the heart of a teenage girl, Ryan sank into his seat, unable to look at his date. *This is the worst. How could I have gotten myself into this mess? This is not the way I wanted to start this relationship.*

Finally, after another groping love scene, Ryan decided, *This is enough. I've got to get Jenni out of here.*

He turned to face her, his face glowing with embarrassment. But she, Kara, and Todd were gone.

Ryan felt like groaning. *They probably went home.*

When he stood to leave, Matt and Dee Ann followed.

"Where'd everyone go?" Dee Ann whispered.

Ryan shook his head, bolting through the double doors. He sighed with relief when he saw Jenni.

"Hi. What are you guys doing out here?" Matt asked.

"We got sick of the movie," Kara confessed to her brother.

Ryan turned to Jenni, "I thought you'd gone home."

Jenni shook her head, "We were waiting."

Grinning, Ryan said, "From now on, instead of hitting a movie we don't know anything about, why don't you come over and watch a nice family video at my house? I make a mean batch of popcorn."

"That sounds great!" Jenni said with a smile.

Kara chimed in, "Maybe we could make a party out of it sometime."

"I'd like that," Ryan said. "I can't think of anything better than a *good* movie, a few friends, and a lot of popcorn."

Help me to pick movies that will not tarnish my spirit. Like a computer, my subconscious retains all images and thoughts that enter my eyes and ears. Help me to turn the switch so I can keep my mind and heart pure for You.

Additional Scripture reading: Philippians 4:4–9

THE
KISS

But the fruit of the Spirit is love, joy, peace, longsuffering, kindness, goodness, faithfulness, gentleness, self-control.—Galatians 5:22–23

Pulling up in front of Jenni's house, Ryan said, "I'm glad we got together tonight. I enjoyed it."

"Me, too," Jenni answered, smiling shyly.

Ryan reached for her, but she pulled away.

"What's wrong?" he asked.

"We don't know each other very well."

"You're right. I'm sorry." He looked at her with admiration. "I want you to know that I respect you."

Jenni pushed away an unruly curl. "You do?"

"After what happened to Shawn and Jackie, I want to avoid physical intimacy."

Nodding, Jenni said, "My guess is, they spent too much time smooching and not enough time talking."

Ryan raised his eyebrows. "That's probably right," he said. "I don't want to fall into that trap." He studied her intensely. "What I really want is to know you better . . . to find out if we can be friends."

"Friends?" Jenni asked. "You mean like buddies?"

Ryan laughed and shook his head and reached for her hand. He winked. "No. Friends, best friends."

Jenni laughed. "Kara's my best friend . . . I don't think you could replace her."

"I don't want to," Ryan explained. "I was more interested in being your best guy."

"I guess I like the sound of that," Jenni admitted. "Still, we have a lot to learn about each other."

Squeezing her hand, he said, "Isn't that what dating's supposed to be about?"

Blushing, Jenni agreed, "I think you're right."

As Ryan walked Jenni to her door, he said, "Tonight was nice. Do you think you'd like to go out again?"

"Sure," Jenni answered.

"I'd like some time just to talk."

"There's always the telephone," Jenni teased. "Just be sure that you're talking to me and not my mom."

Ryan chuckled. "Don't worry," he said. "I promise not to make that mistake twice."

Jenni giggled, "I have to admit, it did make a pretty good impression on Mom. She's still laughing about it."

"Great," Ryan said, rolling his eyes. He looked down at Jenni. *There's something about her expression that seems inviting.*

Closing his eyes, he moved toward her.

For an instant, their lips met. Jenni pushed away. "I've got to go," she said. "Call me."

Lord, the girl issue is a complicated one. Help me develop friendships instead of hot and heavy relationships. Teach me how to get along, how to listen, and how to be a friend. And if there are no Christian girls at my school, please send a revival.

Additional Scripture reading: Galatians 5:16–26

WHAT ELSE?

But grow in the grace and knowledge of
our Lord and Savior Jesus Christ. To Him
be the glory both now and forever. Amen.
—2 Peter 3:18

Later that night, the phone rang. Ryan picked it up. "Hello?"

"Hi, Ryan."

"Eric!" Ryan said. "It's really good to hear your voice. How are you doing?"

"Okay. But I can't talk long," Eric answered.

"How's your rehab going?"

"Good," Eric said. "I'm even starting to be glad you turned me in to Coach."

"You were in over your head."

"I know that now."

"So, how much longer are you going to be at the center?"

"A couple more days. It'll be good to get back home."

"It'll be good to see you," Ryan said.

"When I get out, I'd like to get together with you and ask you some questions."

"Like what?"

"Well, now that I'm a Christian, what do I do?"

"You need to grow in Christ."

"How?"

"By obeying Him, by listening for His voice, by reading His Word, the Bible, and by building relationships with other believers"

"Maybe I could start going to your church," Eric suggested.

"That's a great idea," Ryan said. "I'll introduce you to my youth director, Jeff Hoffman."

Eric's voice tensed. "I'm worried about the guys on the team. What do they think of me now?" he asked.

"They don't know," Ryan said. "The coaches wanted you to be able to start over with a clean sheet."

"Clean?" Eric asked. "I was hardly clean."

"That was the old you," Ryan explained. "If you stick with Christ and avoid tempting situations, you'll be okay."

"Still," Eric said, "I feel like there's something missing. I'm reading the Bible you gave me. And that helps, but what else can I do?"

"Eric, you can't earn God's love. You've got to accept it."

"Didn't you mention that Jesus gave us some commands?" Eric asked. "What are they?"

Lord, I want to obey You. Show me Your commands, and give me the wisdom to follow Your bidding. Help me to always keep in mind that I can't earn Your love. You give it to me freely. I obey You to show my love for You.

Additional Scripture reading: Ephesians 4:11–16

COMMANDS

—

Now he who keeps His commandments abides
in Him, and He in him. And by this we know
that He abides in us, by the Spirit whom He
has given us.—1 John 3:24

"Commands?" Ryan repeated, thumbing through his Bible to Matthew 22:37–40. He read, "Jesus said to him, 'You shall love the LORD your God with all your heart, with all your soul, and with all your mind.' This is the first and great commandment. And the second is like it: 'You shall love your neighbor as yourself.' On these two commandments hang all the Law and the Prophets."

"You mean," Eric challenged, "all Jesus commanded us to do was love Him and love others?"

"There is one more thing," Ryan said, flipping to the last chapter of Mark.

"What?"

"This is something that Jesus said after His death and resurrection. Many people call it His Great Commission."

Ryan scanned the page and began at verse 15: "And He said to them, 'Go into all the world and preach the gospel to every creature. He who believes and is baptized will be saved; but he who does not believe will be condemned.'"

"Baptized? What's that?"

"Baptism is when you get sprinkled or dunked. It's a picture of the death and resurrection of Jesus Christ. It shows the world that your old nature has been buried and you've been made new with Jesus Christ."

"What was it like when you were baptized?" Eric asked.

Ryan hesitated. "Uh, I never was."

"Why not?"

"I don't know. It never came up."

"Does that mean you aren't really a Christian?" Eric asked.

"No. Remember that the thief on the cross was never baptized and Jesus told him, 'Today you will be with Me in Paradise.'"

"Yeah," Eric said with a laugh, "but the thief didn't have any water available. What's your excuse?"

The tips of Ryan's ears reddened. He answered, "I guess I don't have one. I guess I haven't been obedient."

"Maybe when I get out of here," Eric suggested, "the two of us can be baptized together."

Brightening, Ryan said, "Eric, that's a great idea. Maybe we can even talk Todd into getting dunked with us."

"Todd James?"

"Yeah," Ryan said, "he asked Christ to come into his life at youth group."

Eric responded with silence.

"Is something wrong?" Ryan asked.

"No," Eric said, "I was just thinking. Although I don't think Todd is a user, some of his friends from the team are." Eric paused. "I probably shouldn't be saying this, but one even carries a gun."

"A gun?" Ryan said, dropping the receiver. He grabbed for it.

"Yeah, I've seen it in his locker."

"Why would he need a gun?"

"Cocaine is expensive," Eric explained. "Most kids have to steal in order to pay for their habit."

Ryan's jaw dropped. *The robberies at the local convenience stores!* "You don't think that the Masked Bandit is . . . ?"

Eric didn't answer.

"Who do you suspect?" Ryan asked.

"That really wouldn't be fair for me to say," Eric countered. "I have no proof. Besides, it's probably somebody else."

Lord, put a guard on my tongue so I don't spread rumors or lies about others. Teach me to follow Your commandment about

*sharing Your love with others and following You in baptism.
Teach me to love You as well as my neighbors.*

Additional Scripture reading: 1 John 3:13–24

❖

THE MEETING

___

**Watch and pray, lest you enter into temptation.
The spirit indeed is willing, but the flesh is
weak.—Matthew 26:41**

It's interesting how life has changed in the past couple of weeks,
Ryan thought, picking up the phone to call Jenni. *I've got a new
girlfriend, I'm quarterback again, and Eric is getting out of rehab!*

Dialing Jenni's number, he thought about Saturday night's
Homecoming game against MacArthur, the only 5–0 team in the
conference. *I hope we can hold them.*

"Hello, Jenni?"

Mrs. Baker cleared her throat, and Ryan's ears reddened. *Not
again!*

"I'll get her," Mrs. Baker said with a laugh.

As he waited, Ryan thought, *At least I didn't ask her out again.
But if I keep this up, Mrs. Baker will decide I'm some nut, like the
Masked Bandit, and forbid Jenni to go out with me.*

Ryan frowned. *There have been two more robberies since I talked
with Eric. Both times, the getaway vehicle was a red pickup truck
with a blacked-out license plate. I wonder . . .*

"Hi, Ryan," Jenni said, interrupting his thoughts. "I was hoping you'd call."

"What's up?"

"The guys are meeting at Eatza My Pizza to discuss Homecoming night. We're invited."

"Who's going to be there?"

"You know, Kara and Todd, and Dee Ann and Matt."

"That's great. Shall I pick you up?"

"No, Kara and I are getting there early. We've got a lot of catching up to do."

"What time should I meet you?"

"Seven okay?"

"Great."

A few hours later, Ryan scouted the pizzeria.

"Hey, Dee Ann," Ryan called, sliding into the booth. "Congratulations on your nomination for Homecoming queen."

Matt grinned. "She's a shoo-in!"

"Everyone's voting for her!" Kara agreed.

"You're forgetting Brooke," Dee Ann reminded them. "She'd give anything to win the title."

Sniffing, Ryan nodded his head.

Matt shrugged. "I still think you'll win."

"So, what's the plan?" Ryan asked.

"The plan," Todd answered, "is to go on a group date." He winked at Kara. "You know, to keep everyone out of trouble."

Matt sipped his soda. "That's really a great idea," he said, smiling at Dee Ann. "Not that we need a chaperone."

"What exactly is a group date?" Dee Ann asked.

Kara answered, "Well, we'll probably travel together . . ."

"Is that it?" Dee Ann asked.

"No," Kara continued, "we'll sit together at a table at the dance."

"But we're only going to stay at the dance for a little while," Ryan added. "Long enough to show off the new queen. Then we're going over to the church's alternative party, right?"

"Right," Todd agreed.

"Why don't we go a step further?" Matt said. "Why don't we be accountable to each other about our extracurricular activities?"

Jenni looked puzzled. "What do you mean?"

"Let's agree," Matt continued, "not to drink, smoke, do drugs, or take advantage of our dates."

"That sounds like a challenge," Ryan said, smiling at Jenni. "What do you think, Todd?"

Todd grinned at Kara. "Well, I can't say I've ever partied without a beer. But if I can steal a kiss from Kara at her doorstep, I'll consider it."

Reaching for Jenni's hand, Ryan said, "Stealing a kiss sounds like fun. I may have to try that myself."

Please give me Christian friends. Help us to support one another in avoiding temptation. Help us stick together as we grow in You, our perfect Friend.

Additional Scripture reading: Matthew 6:9–15

❖

CRANK CALL

My son, give me your heart,
And let your eyes observe my
ways.—Proverbs 23:26

Saturday morning, Ryan felt restless. *Just jitters over tonight's game,* he decided.

The phone rang, interrupting his solitude. "Hello?" he said.

A muffled voice asked, "Stephens?"

"Who's this?"

The line cracked with what sounded like the cocking of a gun.

"Hello?" Ryan said again.

"You're dead!" the voice announced, moments before the caller banged the receiver in Ryan's ear.

Ryan listened to the dial tone. *That must have been some nut. Although that voice almost sounded like . . . no,* he decided, *I can't let my imagination play tricks on me.*

When Ryan got to the locker room, he ran into Eric. Exchanging high-fives, Ryan said, "Good to have you back!" He ducked, just missing a jock strap as it whizzed past his head.

Looking up, Ryan saw Todd standing on a bench. "This is our night," Todd thundered. "We're gonna whomp the MacArthur Trojans into the dirt!"

The team roared its approval.

"Hey, Ryan!" someone shouted as Ryan pushed his way to his locker. "What's your prediction?"

"We'll kill 'em!" Ryan yelled.

The guys were cheering when Ryan turned to find himself face-to-face with Jack. Jack nodded in agreement. "Dead," he whispered under his breath.

Did I smell alcohol? Ryan wondered, watching Jack swagger away.

As he ran through his pregame warm-ups, Ryan thought through his air and ground strategy. *Even though MacArthur's a powerhouse, I think we can win!*

Ryan shifted uneasily and glanced up, catching Jack's eyes glowering at him like laser beams of hate. *What's his problem?* he wondered, turning away with a shiver.

Straining to touch his toes, Ryan prayed, *This is probably a silly thing to ask, but, Lord, don't leave me now. And, oh, help me to play my best. I give this game to You.*

Lord, please put a hedge of protection around me and my family. Thank You that I can call on You and that You hear me. Keep us safe and show us how to stay on the path You've prepared for us to walk.

Additional Scripture reading: Psalm 27:7–14

THE
GAME

**I thank Christ Jesus our Lord who has enabled
me, because He counted me faithful, putting
me into the ministry.—1 Timothy 1:12**

From his crouched position in the huddle, Ryan could see Jenni
cheering with the squad.

"Ryan, Ryan, Ryan's our man! If he can't do it, no one can!"
they yelled.

Ryan called the play. *The pressure's on!* he thought, moving into
position at MacArthur's twelve-yard line.

The score in the final moments before halftime was 0–0. *So far,*
Ryan thought, *we haven't made our big move, but at least we've
been able to hold MacArthur at bay.*

Ryan checked the clock and his coach. *We've got to use these
final seconds to run one in.*

Following the snap, Ryan faked a handoff to his flanker, watching
MacArthur's line take the bait.

As he rushed forward, Ryan realized, *They haven't figured out
I've got the ball!*

Ryan's cleats showered dirt as he pressed toward the goal line.

Suddenly, a huge linebacker barreled toward him. *Will he stop
me?* Ryan wondered as the linebacker dove for his feet.

Leaping into the air, he twisted out of the linebacker's reach.

Bam! Ryan flew forward as Todd knocked him from behind. He
landed face down in the end zone, still clutching the football.

It's a touchdown! Ryan realized while a grinning Todd helped
him to his feet. The home crowd rose like a giant cloud, cheering
with frenzy.

Later, inside the locker room, Ryan bowed his head. *Thanks,*

Lord, he prayed. *That touchdown meant a lot to me. Thank You for giving me that opportunity.*

Lord, sometimes I take Your love for granted, and I don't even stop to thank You. I'm sorry for that. Help me to always be aware of the part You are playing in my life. I am forever grateful. Thanks!

Additional Scripture reading: 1 Timothy 1:12–17

❖

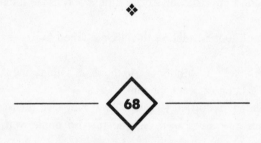

CONFRONTATION

It is honorable for a man to stop
   striving,
Since any fool can start a
   quarrel.—Proverbs 20:3

When Ryan looked up from his prayer, Jack was sitting across from him.

"You must think you're pretty hot stuff," Jack said, sneering.

Rolling his eyes, Ryan said, "Grow up, Jack!"

Jack charged to his feet and grabbed Ryan's jersey. He pulled back his fist. "I ought to—'

"Let go of me!" Ryan demanded, jutting his jaw.

"Why should I?" Jack asked, sneering.

'You're forgetting Coach's rules!"

"So what?" Jack challenged. "I'm already benched. Maybe I should make sure you are, too."

Twisting to free himself, Ryan said, "I'm warning you. I don't want to fight."

"What are you, chicken?"

"No, I'm just not stupid."

The locker room quietened as the players circled the arguing pair.

Ryan ducked and Jack's fist shot past his ear.

Stumbling backward, Ryan yelled, "I said, I'm not going to fight you."

"You don't have a choice," Jack bellowed as he lunged toward Ryan.

Ryan sidestepped Jack as the circle opened to Eric's breathless arrival.

"It's Brooke!" he announced to the team's amazement. "Brooke Kelly's just been crowned queen!"

Grinning, Jack turned to Ryan. "You may own my quarterback position for now, but I own the queen. And unlike you, I'm man enough to keep her happy."

"Good! You deserve each other," Ryan retorted.

Jack started to swing, but Todd caught his arm.

"Whoa!" Todd said. "You need to calm down. We've got a second half to play out there."

Jack cocked his finger like a gun and pointed at Ryan. "I'll even the score later, Quarterbaby."

Eric threw Ryan a warning as Jack stomped away. Eric asked, "What was that all about?"

"I've decided I'm not letting Jack rule my life. From now on, I'm standing up to him."

"Maybe you shouldn't."

"Why not?"

"He's dangerous," Eric said. "I think he's capable of anything."

"What do you mean? He's not the football player with the gun, is he?"

Eric shrugged and said, "What do you think?"

Lord, help me not to just tolerate my enemies but to love them. Help me not to bully but to care. Teach me how to stand up for

You and for myself while I walk away from a fight. Help me remember that sometimes the bravest thing to do is to love instead of slug.

Additional Scripture reading: 2 Timothy 2:22–26

❖

THE VOICE

I will hear what God the LORD will speak.—Psalm 85:8

Jack's got a gun! Ryan realized, trotting back to the field. *I should have figured it out before now. How could I have been so blind?*

Ryan tried to concentrate on the game as cobwebs of fear wove themselves through his mind. *I've got to worry about Jack later,* he finally decided, almost missing the ball at the snap.

Late in the fourth, Ryan groaned as MacArthur scored for 7, gaining the lead by 1 point.

If only John hadn't missed that kick before halftime, Ryan wished, *we would at least be tied.*

Ryan shot off a quick prayer: *Help me, Lord. Coach is letting me make this call. Give me wisdom. Show me what to do.*

He listened quietly. "Try John for a field goal," a gentle voice seemed to whisper.

His eyebrows arched. *Is that You, Lord?* he asked, puzzled. *You're speaking to me about this game?*

Looking toward the sidelines, Ryan thought, *I have to figure this out fast. John still seems shook up over his last miss. Would God want me to give John the chance to try for a twenty-yard field goal?* He flinched at the thought. *I'm not sure what to do. Should I risk it?*

"Trust Me," a gentle voice seemed to answer.

Ryan felt a little queasy, watching John run into position. *I hope I know what I'm doing.*

At the snap, Ryan squinted as John kicked the ball.

Did I miss You, Lord? Ryan prayed as the football veered to the right.

Zing! The ball hit the metal goal post.

Ryan deflated, then gasped. The ball bounced through!

"We won!" Ryan yelled, grabbing John in a huge bear hug.

As he trotted to the sidelines, he smiled. *You know, Lord, winning the game is exciting but not as exciting as knowing that You spoke to me. Thanks.*

Lord, if we only ask and listen, You answer us. Help me to attune my heart to hear Your voice. I know it will take time to recognize You, but teach me. I bind the Enemy from speaking to me in Your stead. Teach me the difference, and help me to know Your voice and not confuse it with the Enemy's or my own voice.

Additional Scripture reading: John 10:1–5

GLOATERS

For You will save the humble people,
But will bring down haughty looks.
—Psalm 18:27

Ryan dressed quickly, watching Jack take a swig from a small flask he had pulled from his locker. *Maybe I can get out of here before there's more trouble,* he thought, grabbing his jacket.

Jumping on a bench, Todd beat his chest in a Tarzan yell. "We're the best!" he screamed.

Ryan dodged a towel fight and slipped into the cool breeze of the parking lot. *There's Jack's truck!*

What had the newspaper said? he wondered. *Oh, yeah. The Masked Bandit's getaway truck had a blacked-out license plate. They said it was like someone had wrapped a dark trash bag around it.*

Glancing over his shoulder, Ryan darted to the rear of the truck and knelt down. *Jack's plate looks clean.*

He slid a finger beneath it. *What's this?* he wondered, yanking off a piece of soft black plastic stuck to some tape. Ryan grimaced as his heart sank. *Jack's the Masked Bandit.*

A voice blared from behind, "What are you doing?"

Jolting upright, Ryan said, "Uh, Todd. Nothing. Just wiping some dirt off."

"Are you crazy? Don't you know that's Jack's truck? If he saw you messing around back here, he'd kill you."

"Look," Ryan said, quickly changing the subject as Jenni and Kara approached. "The girls are coming."

Matt joined them. "Where's Dee?" he asked.

"She'll be here in a minute," Kara said.

Ryan's mind drifted as he thought about Jack. *What should I do? One piece of plastic stuck on the back of a license plate makes for lousy evidence. Is there some way I can prove my theory without getting shot?*

After Dee Ann joined them, he reached for Jenni's hand.

She looked up. "What's wrong?" she asked.

Ryan shook his head and said, "I think there's going to be trouble tonight."

"Trouble?"

Suddenly, Jack and Brooke elbowed their way into the circle of friends. Before Ryan could speak, Jack turned to Matt. "My condolences, Pard. It's too bad you got stuck with a loser!"

"You must be thrilled, Brooke. Congratulations," Dee Ann said.

Brooke cocked her head toward Ryan. She said, "I am, Dee. You don't know what you're missing."

"Uh, are you two going to the dance?" Kara asked.

Jack answered, "Of course, as soon as I get another couple of six-packs."

Before peeling out of the parking lot, Jack turned toward Ryan. He shouted, "I'll even up with you later!"

Touching the piece of plastic he had shoved into his pocket, Ryan shot off a quick prayer: *Don't leave me now, Lord. Show me what to do.*

Thank You for changing my life. Thanks for finding me and giving me a map that keeps me in Your unconditional love. Help me to stay on track, avoiding wrong turns that could lead me into a world of trouble.

Additional Scripture reading: Hebrews 13:5–8

DANCING WITH TROUBLE

God is our refuge and strength,
A very present help in trouble.
—Psalm 46:1

As Ryan and his friends stepped inside the decorated gym, they were greeted by applause. Dee Ann blushed as the crowd cheered. "We love you, Dee Ann!" someone called.

Ryan pulled Jenni to a table and sat down.

"Ryan, you look spooked. Is everything okay?" Jenni asked.

Hesitating, Ryan answered, "I'm not sure. I almost feel like I should stop and pray."

"Pray? Now? You've got to be kidding."

Before Ryan could bow his head, someone yelled, "Dee's queen, regardless of who's wearing the crown!"

Ryan watched Dee Ann brush away a tear. He asked Jenni, "What's going on?"

"There's been some talk that the vote was rigged."

"Rigged?"

Suddenly, the applause and cheering stopped. Ryan looked up to see a scowling Jack standing with Brooke in the gymnasium door.

"What do you think you're doing?" Jack shouted, rushing toward Dee Ann. "Brooke's the queen, not you, you little cow!"

Ryan froze, watching Matt step in between Dee Ann and Jack. *Will Jack pull his gun?* he wondered. He rose to his feet and grabbed Jenni's hand. "We've got to get out of here."

He led Jenni and Dee Ann to the door, then went back for Matt,

Todd, and Kara. He saw two adult chaperons running toward the group.

Jack threw a fist at Matt. "I'll teach you!" he roared, stumbling to the floor. Turning, Jack growled, "Why, you—"

"Jack, you're drunk!" Matt yelled. "Too drunk to fight!" Jack charged again, thudding into Matt and hammering a fist into his head.

Matt smacked his fist into Jack's stomach. As Jack slipped to the floor, Matt addressed the crowd, "Sorry to stop the show, but beating up drunks just isn't my style."

Ryan pushed Matt to the door and said, "We've got to get out of here."

The door slammed behind them, and Jack yelled to their unhearing ears, "I'll get you for this! We'll settle this tonight!"

The world brings trouble, but You bring us blessings. Give me the power to share Your blessings with others. Teach me how to lead my friends out of the world's pain and into Your loving embrace.

Additional Scripture reading: Psalm 10:1–15

THE CRASH

Make no friendship with an angry man,
And with a furious man do not go,
Lest you learn his ways
And set a snare for your soul.
—Proverbs 22:24–25

Ryan and Jenni were halfway to their car when the gym door burst open. Jack charged out, dragging Brooke behind him. Brooke held the crown onto her head and screamed, "Run! Jack's got a gun!"

"Hurry!" Ryan demanded, pulling Jenni through the parking lot. Her eyes wide, Jenni asked, "Jack's got a *what?*"

Ryan pushed Jenni into the car. He climbed in after her and slammed the door behind them. His foot reached for the gas while his fingers fumbled with the keys. *I'm glad Kara and Todd decided to ride with Matt and Dee. They've already made it out of the parking lot.*

Racing his engine, Ryan riveted his eyes to his rearview mirror. He could see Jack pulling Brooke into the cab of his truck. *Why doesn't she try to get away from that creep?*

Jack's lights blinked like an awakening giant as his engine roared to life. "We've got to get out of here!" Ryan muttered, turning his car onto the street. Jack lurched his truck toward the exit, suddenly swerving to avoid another car.

He's drunk! Blind drunk! Ryan realized as Jack's truck barreled over the curb toward them. He stepped on the gas in an attempt to avoid being broadsided.

Inside the cab of the pickup, a flash of silver glinted under the streetlights.

Jenni screamed as the blast of the gunshot competed with the clash of the colliding vehicles.

As metal twisted through metal, Ryan lost his grip on the steering wheel, and the world spun out of control.

"Jenni?" Ryan finally called into the silence. There was no answer. He reached for her. Her seat was empty. He tried to speak, but his voice caught in his throat.

Where is she? What's happened? Before he could look, the streetlights faded to black.

Help me avoid close friendships with angry people. If anger seeps into my heart, help me identify it and turn it over to You. Help me take advantage of every opportunity to share Your love with others.

Additional Scripture reading: Proverbs 23:17–21

❖

73

THE AFTERMATH

But may the God of all grace, who called us to
His eternal glory by Christ Jesus, after you
have suffered a while, perfect, establish,
strengthen, and settle you.—1 Peter 5:10

The glow of the streetlights slowly returned. *Jenni!* Ryan remembered. *Where is she?*

He pushed open his car door. He could see Jack was out cold, crumpled against his steering wheel. *Does he still have his gun?* Ryan wondered.

Ryan staggered toward Jack's truck. *The passenger door's ajar,* he noticed through a blur. *Where's Brooke?*

He stumbled into her body. Catching his balance, he stared down at her. Her neck was twisted at an odd angle, and blood trickled out of one of her ears. *Brooke's neck is broken!*

Emergency lights flashed as paramedics scrambled toward them. "Out of our way," they shouted. Kara, Matt, and Dee Ann stepped back.

Ryan lifted the back of his hand to his forehead. It felt wet and sticky. *I'm covered with blood!* he noticed with surprise. Kara hugged him, "Ryan! Are you okay?"

The streetlights swayed. Ryan reached out to her for support. "I . . . I think so. Where's Jenni?"

Kara pointed to the paramedics who were hoisting Jenni onto a stretcher. Blood flowed from a gash in Jenni's head. *A gunshot wound?* Ryan wondered.

He stumbled toward her. "Jenni? Are you all right?" he called.

Jenni's eyes fluttered, and a woman grabbed Ryan's shoulders. "I don't know if you believe in prayer. But if you do, pray now. We found your friend in the middle of the road. Apparently, she went through the windshield. It's hard to know how bad she's hurt."

Especially if Jack shot her, Ryan thought, teetering backward. He landed on his bottom. The woman leaned over him. "You don't look so good," she said, handing him her hanky to press against his head wound. She called, "This boy needs help!"

Trying to focus, Ryan wondered, *How could this have happened? Where was God?*

Things happen in life, things that are hard to understand. Sometimes I wonder if You even care. Yet, somehow I know You do. You are with us when tragedy strikes. You give us peace as we battle through life. Thank You for being there. Thank You that I can always turn to You.

Additional Scripture reading: Revelation 21:1–4

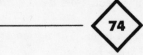

BY
AMBULANCE

___

But Jesus said, "Let the little children come to
Me, and do not forbid them; for of such is the
kingdom of heaven."—Matthew 19:14

A paramedic sat down next to Ryan and shone a flashlight into
his eyes.

"Can you walk?" he asked.

Ryan nodded. "I think so."

"Good. You can sit in the ambulance that's about to leave, the
one with the girl from the red truck."

"You mean Brooke?"

"Do you know her?" the paramedic asked. "Maybe you could
help us reach her parents when we get to the hospital."

Stumbling toward the ambulance, Ryan climbed inside and sat
next to Brooke's gurney. *She's still conscious. Maybe she's going to
be all right!*

Brooke looked up at him. A tear trickled down her cheek.

"It's bad, Ryan. Really bad," she said.

"You don't know that," Ryan said, wishing his words sounded
more assuring.

"I can't move. I can't feel anything."

Ryan reached down and stroked her hair. "Can I pray for you?"

"Would you?" Brooke asked. "I don't know how."

Bowing his head, Ryan tried to clear his mind. *Is Brooke paralyzed?*

"Who are you praying to?" Brooke asked.

"Jesus," Ryan replied.

"I heard about Him in Vacation Bible School once. He's the
One who asked that the children come to Him, right?"

"Yes," Ryan answered, his eyes wide. *Doesn't she know Him?*

Brooke's pupils dilated into black pools. She asked, "If I die tonight, do you think I could go to Him?"

"You're not going to die," Ryan said hoarsely.

"Maybe. But I want to be sure," Brooke replied. "Please tell me how I can be one of His children."

Hesitating, Ryan tried to focus. "Give Him your life. He'll give you His love and forgiveness."

Closing her eyes, Brooke sighed a prayer: "Jesus, it's me, Brooke. Would You take me just as I am? I want to be Yours. Forgive me for not asking sooner."

"Everything is going to be okay," Ryan said. "You're in God's hands now."

Lord, there is nothing You can't forgive. Help me to live my life in such a way that my regrets will be few and my life will be whole. Thank You for forgetting my sins while remembering me with Your love.

Additional Scripture reading: Romans 3:23–27

WHERE'S GOD?

Though He slay me, yet will I trust
Him.—Job 13:15

Ryan lay in his hospital bed. His mother had already gone home. *What will Dad say when he finds out? He's probably out of town again,* he decided. *Figures. He's never around when I really need him.*

Ryan turned his face to the wall. *Just when I thought I was getting my life under control, this had to happen.* He sighed. *The worst thing about this whole situation is not knowing how the others are. Sure, the doctor said I'll be okay. I'll probably go home in the morning. But what about Jenni? What about Brooke?*

A voice called, "Ryan, the nurse said you were still awake. May I come in?"

Turning, Ryan saw Pastor Jeff standing in the doorway.

"Oh, hi. I'm glad you came."

Jeff sat next to his bed. "How are you feeling?" he asked.

"A little worse than my one-and-only hangover," Ryan admitted, gently touching his bandaged head.

"You weren't drinking tonight, were you?"

Shaking his head, Ryan said, "No, my friends and I made a pledge not to do that."

"Good."

Ryan said, "Too bad Jack didn't swear off the booze. Is there any word on his condition?"

"He's stable."

Anger flushed Ryan's face. "Figures," he said. "Jack's the villain who always gets away."

"Not this time."

"What do you mean?"

"His alcohol content was pretty high. Plus, with the other stuff they found . . ."

"Stuff?"

"His gun and mask."

Ryan nodded.

"You don't seem too surprised."

"He was pointing that gun in my direction when we crashed. I'm afraid he shot Jenni. Have you heard anything?"

Jeff shook his head.

"So, is he in big trouble?" Ryan asked, his eyes shining with hope.

"Could be, especially if they charge him with manslaughter."

"Jenni! Is she . . ."

"She's still unconscious."

"Is she going to be okay?"

"They don't know yet. But everyone seems more worried about Brooke."

"Brooke? But she was alert in the ambulance."

"Her brain has started to swell, and they think her neck is broken. They just put her on life support. It doesn't look good."

"Why?" Ryan asked. "Why did this happen? Where's God in this?"

God, sometimes it seems the world is falling apart, and I have to wonder, Where are You? Yet, I know You can take the broken threads of people's lives and weave them into beautiful designs. Design my life in a way that will glorify You.

Additional Scripture reading: John 14:1–15

❖

THE REASON

And we know that all things work together
for good to those who love God, to those
who are the called according to His purpose.
—Romans 8:28

"*Why* is a hard question," Jeff responded. "Let me ask you a question."

"What?" Ryan asked.

"Why did you go out for football?"

"I don't know. It was something I always wanted to do."

"Did God force you to try out?"

"No, I don't think I even consulted Him," Ryan responded.

"Well, it's the same thing with the accident."

"What do you mean?"

"Jack was in charge of making his own choices. Unfortunately, his choices resulted in tragic consequences."

"I'm not following you."

"Think about it," Jeff said. "Did anyone at the Homecoming dance force Jack to drink?"

"No."

"The drinking was his choice?"

"I guess so."

"Did anyone force Jack to chase you with his truck?"

"He was mad. He wanted to get even."

"Even Jack's response to his anger was his choice."

"What are you getting at?"

"My point is, God never forces His ways on us. We make our own choices."

"I get it," Ryan said. "The accident was caused by Jack, not by God."

"That's right. We can't blame God when things go wrong. Our choices, as well as the choices of others, can have powerful consequences."

Reddening, Ryan said, "You're saying this is all Jack's fault."

"And what's your response to that?" Jeff asked.

"I'd like to kill him," Ryan replied. "He had no right to do what he did."

"True, but would killing Jack make everything all right?"

"No. I'd probably have to go to jail."

"Jail terms are often the consequence of murder," Jeff replied. "But can't you think of a better response to Jack?"

"Like what?"

"Like forgiving him."

Ryan's jaw dropped. "Jack doesn't deserve my forgiveness!"

"True, but do you deserve God's forgiveness?"

"Well, no."

"But didn't God demand that we forgive others?"

"He didn't mean people like Jack, did He?"

"What do you think?"

"Maybe, but it doesn't seem right." Ryan looked puzzled.

"That could be, but God has a reason for asking us to forgive."

"What?"

"When we forgive others, we free ourselves from anger and bitterness," Jeff said.

Ryan was silent. "At least that gives me something to think about," he said. "But I still don't get it. I mean, Jack's caused so much pain."

"He has," Jeff agreed. "But don't you think God is big enough to take this tragedy and turn it into something good?"

"I don't know. Can He?" Ryan asked.

"The Scripture says He can, and He will," Jack replied.

Lord, sometimes I don't think my choices matter. Help me realize my choices have consequences. I know You will always forgive me, but You may require me to live with the consequences of choices made by and for me. Teach me to live for You.

Additional Scripture reading: Ephesians 6:10–18

JENNI'S DISCOVERY

Reckon yourselves to be dead indeed to sin,
but alive to God in Christ Jesus our Lord.
—Romans 6:11

The next morning, Ryan slipped into his clothes. *I'm glad to be going home. Lying in a hospital bed gives me too much time to think. It's no wonder I have a headache.* He put his wallet into his pocket. *But I guess I should consider myself lucky. I just hope Jenni and Brooke are as fortunate. If only there were some news.*

Looking into the bathroom mirror, Ryan remembered Jeff's words. *It seems impossible to forgive someone like Jack,* Ryan thought with a frown. *But doesn't the Bible say all things are possible with God?*

I still can't figure out how to forgive Jack. He doesn't deserve it, and I doubt he even wants it, Ryan thought, reaching for a paper towel.

When Ryan stepped into the hallway, he almost ran into Mrs. Baker.

"How's Jenni?" he asked.

"You're the first to know!" she said, smiling. "She came out of her coma this morning. They've just wheeled her out of ICU."

"That's great!"

"We're not spreading it around yet," Mrs. Baker said. "She needs to rest, but why don't you go see her? A visit from you might be just what the doctor ordered."

Ryan tapped on Jenni's door.

"Come in," a groggy voice answered.

Ryan pulled up a chair and studied Jenni's pale face. "How are you feeling?"

She touched her bandaged head, then touched Ryan's. "Like we were crowned king and queen of the Homecoming dance," she said.

"Well, it's good to see you have a sense of humor."

"I'm just glad to be alive. When I saw Jack's gun, I thought we were going to die."

Gently touching her bandage, Ryan asked, "Were you hit?"

"No. This crown covers a cut I got from hitting the windshield."

"That's good, I guess," Ryan replied.

Jenni asked, "Are Jack and Brooke okay?"

Ryan shook his head, unwilling to share the bad news. "I really don't know."

"It's too bad Jack doesn't know God," Jenni lamented.

"What do you mean?" Ryan asked, raising his eyebrows.

"Well, if he knew who he could be in Christ, maybe he wouldn't be so angry all the time."

"Who he could be in Christ?" Ryan asked.

"Yeah," Jenni responded. "Kara and I have been memorizing a list."

"A list? What kind of list?"

"Traits God uses to describe us Christians."

"Traits? Like what?"

Jenni touched her head. "It's hard to think. Let's see, when we're in Christ, we're accepted and significant."

Intrigued, Ryan said, "Yeah?"

"And we're justified and can have peace."

"Peace?" Ryan asked.

"Yes, we're forgiven, and we have God's grace and the spirit of power, love, and self-discipline."

"I never realized all that," Ryan said, noticing Jenni was tiring. "I'll come back later, and we'll talk some more. Right now, I'm going to see what I can find out about Jack and Brooke."

(To be prayed aloud.) *Lord Jesus, please come into my life. Forgive me of my sins, and be my Lord.*

Thank You that Your Word says I am a new creature and a child of God. I am delivered from the power of darkness and transferred into God's kingdom. I am redeemed and blessed. I am strong and more than a conqueror. I am the light of the world and the salt of the earth. I am righteous and God lives in me. I have the power of the Holy Spirit, and this power is greater than the power of the Enemy, so I can do all things through Christ who strengthens me. As Your ambassador, I will tell the good news to others. But most of all, Lord, thank You that You will never leave me or forsake me.

Additional Scripture reading: Romans 6:20–23

BRITTLE LEAF

Blessed is the man
Who walks not in the counsel of
   the ungodly, . . .
But his delight is in the law of the
   LORD. . . .
He shall be like a tree
Planted by the rivers of water, . . .
Whose leaf also shall not wither.
    —Psalm 1:1–3

Ryan lay on the couch while his mom and sister spoke in hushed tones in the kitchen. He could just make out what they were saying.

Kristi said, "The police found cocaine in Jack's truck. Plus, they found his mask and gun. They think Jack's the Masked Bandit."

"That's hard to believe," Mrs. Stephens replied.

"Why? Jack's a jerk," Kristi said, raising her voice.

"He's a troubled young man," her mom replied. "He comes from a broken home."

"Like that's an excuse? I don't want to remind you, but I come from a broken home, too."

"I know the divorce has been hard on you," Mrs. Stephens replied.

"Hard?" Kristi asked. "It's been a nightmare . . . one that won't stop. Things went from bad to worse when Jack entered the picture."

"Kristi, you can't let what Jack did to you hold you back. You've got to move forward."

"Move forward? How can I move forward when I feel like I'm about to explode?"

"Why do you feel like that?"

"Because I hate my life and I hate Jack."

"Don't say that," Mrs. Stephens said. "Hate will only hurt you. It won't solve your problems."

"My whole life is a problem," Kristi complained. "I wish I'd never been born!"

Ryan blinked as he heard the sound of the kitchen door slam. *Ever since the rape, Kristi's emotions have been surging out of control.*

Rubbing his head, he thought, *And who can blame her? Things have been rough.*

He stood up and stretched. *It's weird to see Kristi so emotional when she was once so bubbly. Dad's leaving was hard, but Jack's abuse seems to be pushing her over the edge.*

As Ryan approached the kitchen, he realized, *Kristi is helping me see Jeff's point. Hate and bitterness destroy the hater.*

"Hi, Mom. Are you okay?"

Mrs. Stephens nodded, dabbing a tissue to her eyes. "I don't know what to do about Kristi," she said. "I thought she was doing better when she found out that her AIDS test was negative. I guess I'm not sure if I can help her."

"Let me try and talk to her, Mom," Ryan said, reaching for the door handle. He found Kristi slumped on the back porch, staring at a dead leaf.

Sitting next to her, Ryan asked, "How are you doing?"

"How do you think?" Kristi muttered.

"I know the past few weeks have been hard. But hating Jack won't make things better."

"It feels good," Kristi replied.

"Really?"

Kristi shrugged.

Ryan said, "I've been thinking. I've decided hate poisons the hater, not the hated."

Kristi didn't answer.

"Have you ever wondered why Jesus made such a big deal out of forgiving others?" Ryan asked.

Kristi shook her head.

"Once, I thought He meant we should forgive the people we

could excuse . . . you know, people who had a nice reason for their goof-ups."

"That leaves Jack out. There's no excuse for him."

"That's my point. Even though Jack is inexcusable, he's still forgivable."

"How can you say that?"

"It's like this. Jesus knows hate dries our spirits. That's why He wants us to forgive everyone, excuse or no excuse."

Ryan reached for the leaf and crumpled it in his hand. "Bitterness makes us brittle. It keeps us from knowing God."

"So, what do we do?" Kristi asked, folding her arms. "Pretend like everything's all right?"

"No, we need to forgive others, no matter what. We need to give our hurts to God and let Him carry them. That's when God can turn our hurts into good."

Kristi stared at him. "Are you willing to forgive Jack?"

"I'm thinking about it."

"Are you going to do it in person?"

"I don't know."

"Well, if you decide to go see him, I'd like to be there."

"Why?"

"Because I don't think you can forgive Jack. I think Jack'll badger you until you smash his face in." Kristi's eyes gleamed. "I want to be there to watch."

Lord, help me to be free from my stubborn pride. Not only is it hard to seek forgiveness, it can be hard to forgive. I give my unforgiveness to You. Soften it with Your love, and give me the strength to love and forgive my enemies.

Additional Scripture reading: Matthew 5:1–12

MOUNTAIN CLIMBING

Many people shall come and say,
"Come, and let us go up to the mountain
of the LORD,
To the house of the God of Jacob;
He will teach us His ways,
And we shall walk in His paths."
—Isaiah 2:3

Ryan and Kristi had spent the morning in the police station answering questions and filling out forms.

After grabbing some lunch, they walked to the hospital.

"Ryan, there you are," Jeff said. "I'm glad I caught you. Do you have a moment?"

Ryan nodded as Kristi said, "I'm going to get a drink of water."

Ryan and Jeff sat down in a couple of chairs outside surgery.

"How are you feeling?" Jeff asked.

"Better. Especially now that I've decided to confront Jack."

Jeff arched a brow. "Oh?"

"Can you believe it? I'm actually going to try to forgive him."

"Good for you."

"I feel better than I have in a month."

"How are you doing otherwise? Are you still considering whether or not to be president of our youth council?"

"Maybe, but I'm still not sure if I'm ready for that kind of responsibility."

"Why not?"

"I'm still trying to know God."

"What do you mean?"

"It's kind of like that climb I took with Kristi and Dad. I keep thinking that I'm almost close enough to touch God, that I'll see His face around the next bend. But then, God seems as far away as ever."

"Let me ask you a question," Jeff said. "When you look for God, does He seem like a mountain peak in the distance, or does He seem like a peak hidden in the clouds?"

"I guess He's more like a peak hidden in the clouds," Ryan admitted. "I know I'm close, but I don't seem quite able to reach Him."

"That's good."

"Good?"

"Sure," Jeff said. "When you first decided to follow the Lord, the journey seemed impossible. It seemed like a distant mountain stretching before you in the distance, right?"

"Yeah."

"Think about it. You've hiked so far, you're no longer viewing God from a distance. You're actually climbing His mountain. In fact, you may be nearing the top."

"How can I tell?"

"Instead of looking up, look down. Are you at the same height you were in your Christian walk a month ago?"

Shaking his head, Ryan said, "No. I'm higher."

"Don't you think that's good?"

"Maybe, but why do I feel so frustrated?"

"The Holy Spirit is nudging you to climb higher."

"Will I ever get to the top?" Ryan asked.

"Our Christian walk is a journey. It lasts a lifetime."

Wilting, Ryan said, "Then there's no hope."

"No hope?" Jeff asked. "Haven't you figured out who your climbing partner is?"

Ryan shook his head.

"It's the Lord Jesus Himself. He's with you every step of the way. And as He promised, He'll never leave you or forsake you."

"But I wanted to stand on the uppermost peak. I wanted to talk to Him face-to-face."

"That will come," Jeff promised. "But in the meantime, enjoy your journey. It's an adventure."

"Is there anything I can do to speed it up?"

"Have you let go?" Jeff asked.

"Let go?"

"Yes," Jeff nodded. "Let go of your life and give it to God."

"But didn't I do that when I became a Christian?"

"Giving God your sins and your heart isn't the same as giving Him your life. That's the next step."

Ryan smiled. "I'll do it," he said.

"Does that mean you're going to join the youth council?" Jeff asked.

"Let me pray about it," Ryan said with a smile. "I'm ready to do whatever God asks."

Although my climb toward You is sometimes difficult, You are with me. You go before me and blaze a trail for me to follow. Help me not to get lost in the clouds but to realize I'm on a continuing adventure with You. Give me strength and stamina to make it to the top. And help me forgive others as You have forgiven me.

Additional Scripture reading: Proverbs 4:10–22

FREE!

For this is God,
Our God forever and ever;
He will be our guide
Even to death.—Psalm 48:14

Kristi stood trembling at the door to Jack's hospital room. "Are you sure you want to go in there? You don't have to, you know," Ryan said. "Jack's liable to say anything."

Nodding, Kristi declared, "I *want* to face him."

Ryan tapped gently on the door. "I kinda hope he's asleep."

"Who's there?" Jack bellowed.

"It's me, Ryan. If you're busy, I can leave," Ryan said, sticking his head in the door.

Jack glared. "Who's behind you?" he asked.

"It's my sister, Kristi."

"Oh, yes. Kris, the dish."

Kristi sniffed indignantly as Ryan said, "Uh, maybe I should come back later."

"No," Jack said, propping himself up on one elbow. "I'm surprised you had the guts to show your face. Especially after the trouble you caused last night."

Stiffening, Ryan said, "The trouble *I* caused?"

"If you and your stupid friends had let Brooke enjoy her crown, I wouldn't have lost my temper."

Tentatively, Ryan stepped forward as Kristi shadowed him. *Lord,* Ryan prayed, *I came to forgive Jack, but how?*

"I'm sorry about that," Ryan said. "I thought Brooke made a beautiful Homecoming queen."

A look of sorrow flashed across Jack's face. "How is Brooke? Do you know?"

"The last I heard, she was in a coma."

"Oh." Jack's sorrow chilled into a sneer. He turned to Kristi. "So," he asked, "why are *you* here?" He gave her the once-over. "Did you come back for more?"

"No. My brother has something to say to you. Shut up and listen," Kristi snapped, stomping her foot.

Jack rolled his eyes from Kristi to Ryan. "This ought to be good."

Ryan stepped closer. "I came to tell you I don't hate you anymore."

Snorting, Jack cocked his head. "What a relief," he growled.

"There's been a lot of bad blood between us. I'm sorry for my part in it. I want you to know I forgive you," Ryan said.

"Oh, goody."

"But my forgiveness does not entitle you to hurt me or my sister. In fact, we were at the police station this morning. We filed a report on Kristi's rape. Although we forgive you, you'll still have to face the consequences of your actions. You'll be hearing from the police soon."

"I'm quaking in my boots."

Kristi stepped out from behind Ryan. "Whether you know it or not, or whether you even care, you hurt me. For a while, I just wanted to see you dead. But now . . . now I feel sorry for you."

Jack slapped his thigh. "Gee, I'm really touched."

Grabbing Kristi by the hand, Ryan said, "We're leaving. But before we go, we just want you to know we'll be praying for you."

"Don't bother," Jack retorted. "I don't need your self-righteousness."

"I'm sorry you feel that way," Ryan said. "But know this. Kristi and I are free of you. And we are going to pray for you from a distance."

Thank You for providing a way for us to be free through Your forgiveness. And thank You for providing a way for me to forgive others. Help me to keep myself free of obstacles to my freedom.

Additional Scripture reading: John 8:31–36

❖

RELEASED FROM BONDAGE!

—

For if you forgive men their trespasses, your
heavenly Father will also forgive you. But if
you do not forgive men their trespasses,
neither will your Father forgive your
trespasses.—Matthew 6:14–15

Ryan led Kristi out of Jack's hospital room and asked, "How do you feel?"

"It's funny," Kristi replied. "I feel better than I have since the rape."

"I feel better, too," Ryan admitted.

"Do you think our hate for Jack will come back to haunt us?"

"Probably," Ryan replied. "Especially if he continues to annoy us."

Nodding, Kristi said, "Ryan, you were great in there. I'm impressed."

Ryan grinned. "That speech took everything I had. I almost slugged Jack, despite my good intentions."

"Why didn't you?" Kristi asked.

"I don't know. I guess I was trying to obey God."

"How can we stay free of Jack?"

"I'm not sure. All I know is, I'm going to try to stay away from him."

"That's not a bad idea. But what if his lawyers get him off? What if he goes out for basketball? What are you going to do then?"

"Jack's in big trouble. I doubt he'll get off so easily," Ryan said. "But if he does, I guess I'll have to pray a lot and turn my feelings over to God. As far as I'm concerned, I'm only supposed to be willing to forgive. God's in charge of everything else."

An overhead loudspeaker sputtered to life. A voice announced, "Code Blue! ICU-B! Code Blue! ICU-B!"

Kristi gasped as doctors and nurses charged down the hall. "What's happening?" she asked.

"It's an emergency of some kind," Ryan said. "Someone in the Intensive Care Unit is in serious trouble."

"I wonder who?"

Ryan froze. "Brooke's in ICU-B."

Thank You for giving me the opportunity to be free from those who have wronged me. Sometimes my hate and unforgiveness are too big for me to handle. But You have provided a way. When I'm willing, You give the power to forgive. And when unforgiveness tries to revisit me, You are there to help me forgive again and again. Thank You.

Additional Scripture reading: Matthew 18:21–35

❖

82

HEALED!

For if we live, we live to the Lord; and if we
die, we die to the Lord. Therefore, whether we
live or die, we are the Lord's.—Romans 14:8

By the time Ryan and Kristi rounded the corner to the ICU waiting room, it was over. They found Kara grieving in a corner. Rushing to her side, Ryan asked, "What's happened?"

"It's Brooke," she said, "she's gone."

The news cut Ryan like a knife. "That can't be right," he said.

"Her mom just told me," Kara said with a sniffle.

Ryan slumped into a chair. *This isn't fair,* he thought. *Brooke was so young, so beautiful. She didn't deserve this.*

"I was hoping God would heal her," he finally said.

Jeff walked across the room and sat beside him. "Maybe He did."

"But she's dead. How could she be healed?"

"Do you think she knew Jesus?" Jeff asked.

Nodding, Ryan said, "She met Him last night. The last thing she said to me was, 'If He calls me, I will go.'"

"Really?" Kara asked. "That just confirms my experience with her."

"What's that?"

"Earlier today, when I talked to her about God, she roused from her coma as if she was trying to send me a signal. Now I'm certain she's with Him."

"That's good," Ryan said. "But I guess I really failed her."

"Why do you say that?" Jeff asked.

"Well, last night, when she asked me to pray for her, she didn't even know to whom I prayed. I dated her all summer and never told her about the Lord."

Jeff put his arm around Ryan's shoulders. "In moments like this you realize how important it is that we share our faith. Don't you see? Even if you missed an opportunity last summer, God used you anyway."

Kristi asked, "Why did you say Brooke might be healed now that she's gone?"

"She's no longer a prisoner of her body," Jeff explained. "She's with the Lord. I can't think of anything more wonderful than that."

"If it's so wonderful," Ryan asked, "why do you pray for people who are sick? Why don't you offer them euthanasia?"

"Euthanasia? What's that?" Kristi asked.

"Euthanasia is what some people call mercy killing. I call it murder," Jeff said. "Remember what Paul said in Philippians 1:21? 'For to me, to live is Christ, and to die is gain.'

"My point is this: Death is not the worst thing that can happen to a person. But we have to remember, God is big enough to take a life, in His time. But it's not right for us to rush things that aren't meant to be rushed. That would be interfering in God's plans and purpose for us and our loved ones."

"Are you saying we should never let a loved one die?" Ryan asked.

"As Ecclesiastes says, 'To everything there is a season, a time for every purpose under heaven.' Even a time to die. I'm not for prematurely rushing the dying process, but neither am I for keeping brain-dead people hooked to machines. There's a balance, a balance that must be carefully sought and kept."

Ryan sighed. "I see what you mean. God has a purpose for all of us, even people who are sick," he said.

"That's right. We need to trust Him. We need to rejoice when He heals our bodies, but we also need to rejoice when He takes our loved ones home to be with Him."

You are the Alpha and the Omega. You are the first and the last. Although our lives are as brief gusts of wind that rustle the grass for an instant, You care for us. You know and care about our lives and our deaths. Help me respect the lives You've created—the very new, the vibrant, the frail, and the weak. Be in control of my passage through this world, and help me respect the passages of others.

Additional Scripture reading: 1 Corinthians 15:51–58

THE
LAST DREAM

—

If I take the wings of the morning,
And dwell in the uttermost parts of the sea,
Even there Your hand shall lead me,
And Your right hand shall hold me.
—Psalm 139:9–10

Ryan climbed into his bed and closed his eyes. A mountain slowly rose beneath him. He looked at the sun glowing through the clouds just above his head. I've come a long way, *he realized.*

He looked down. A rope hung limply from his waist. Where's Jack? *he wondered.* I thought we were on belay.

A soft breeze swirled around him. He could hear the voice of his Lord. "You are free."

An eagle soared past him. It was Jack! *He flew downward, just skimming the trees.*

The Lord spoke, "He's still bound to the earth. He's not ready to experience My love."

Another eagle soared toward a break in the clouds. It's Brooke! *Ryan realized.*

"I'm free!" *she sang as the clouds encompassed her.*

"Now what, Lord?" *Ryan prayed.*

"I am with you. Do not be afraid. I am your God."

"But don't I need to let go?" *Ryan asked.*

"You already have," *the Lord's voice spoke warmly.* "I have you in the palm of My hand."

Ryan looked down. No longer was he clinging to the edge of a perilous cliff. He was secure in the Lord's hand.

"Rest now," *the Lord told him.* "You have a long climb ahead of you."

"Climb?" Ryan asked. "Where are we going?"

"Trust Me."

"I will," Ryan said, drifting off to sleep. "I will follow You, no matter where You lead."

Before Ryan closed his eyes, he noticed the clouds above him were beginning to look stormy.

No matter. I am with God.

Not only, Lord, have You given me wings of freedom, but You've given me shelter from storms. Help me to keep climbing toward You. I commit all of my ways to You. Thank You for not only being aware of me but allowing me to know You.

Additional Scripture reading: Ephesians 3:14–21

❖

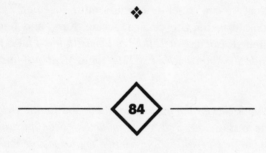

BAPTISM

> And now why are you waiting? Arise and be
> baptized, and wash away your sins, calling on
> the name of the Lord.—Acts 22:16

"Ryan, do you follow your Lord in baptism?" Jeff asked. Ryan nodded, his body still adjusting to the coolness of the water.

"Can you tell the congregation why you've chosen to step into these waters?"

Trying to stop his chattering teeth, Ryan cleared his throat. "I do this in obedience to my Lord Jesus," he said. "He has taken away my sins, and He has taken control of my life. I do this to show the world how much I love Him."

Jeff smiled. "Then, Ryan Wayne Stephens, I baptize you in the name of the Father, the Son, and the Holy Spirit. I baptize you into Jesus' life, death, and resurrection."

Ryan closed his eyes, allowing Jeff to lean him into the cool water. Moments later, as his head broke the surface, he raised his hands in victory.

The congregation applauded. Turning, Ryan caught sight of his dad standing near the back door. *He's here!*

As he sloshed his way out of the baptismal tank, he reached for his friends, Todd and Eric. *This is a good day,* he realized, giving each one a wet bear hug.

Eric wiped his damp hair out of his eyes. "Thanks for introducing me to the Lord," he said, shivering in his damp robe.

"It's great we can travel on our adventure together," Todd said as each took turns hugging Shawn, Jackie, Kara, and Jenni.

Ryan smiled. *Not only will the Lord be with me, I have two more good friends to share with. Exciting times wait just around the corner.*

> *Lord, thank You for the trials, and thank You for the victories. Help me to stay close, and teach me how to hear Your voice. I continue to give myself to You. Thank You for giving Yourself to me. Thank You for the adventures waiting for me to enter into them. Amen.*

Additional Scripture reading: Romans 6:1–11